Kaplan Publishing are constantly fi
ways to make a difference to you
exciting online resources really d
different to students looking for e

This book comes with free MyKaplan online resources so that you can study anytime, anywhere

Having purchased / materials:

CONTENT		FIA (excluding FFA,FAB,FMA)	
		Text	Kit
iPaper version of the book		✓	✓
Interactive electronic version			
Progress tests with instant a			
Mock assessments online			
Material updates		✓	✓
Latest official ACCA exam qu			
Extra question assistance us			
Timed questions with an onl			
Interim assessment includin		✓	
Technical articles		✓	✓

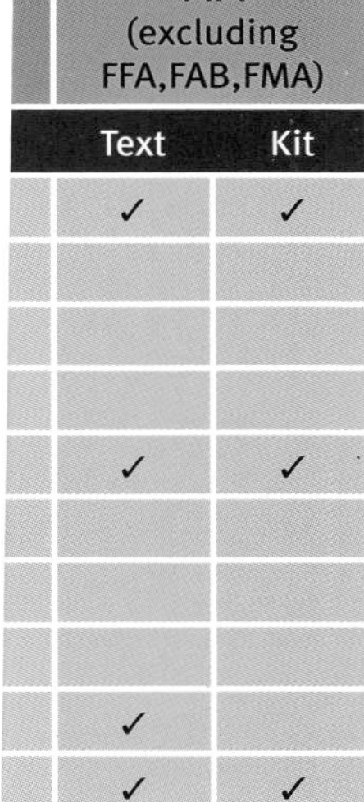

* Excludes F1, F2, F3, FFA, FAE

How to access you

Kaplan Financial stude ... vill be available to you online ... hen you enrolled. If you are having proble

If you are already a re ... the 'add a book' feature and ent ... n of this card. Then click 'finished' or 'add ... rom this screen.

If you purchased throu ... will automatically receive an e-mail invit ... n access to your conten ... an Flexible Learning.

If you are a new MyKaplan user register at www.MyKaplan.co.uk and click on the link contained in the email we sent you to activate your account. Then select the 'add a book' feature, enter the ISBN number of this book and the unique pass key at the bottom of this card. Then click 'finished' or 'add another book'.

Your Code and Information

This code can only be used once for the registration of one book online. This registration and your online content will expire when the final sittings for the examinations covered by this book have taken place. Please allow one hour from the time you submit your book details for us to process your request.

Please scratch the film to access your MyKaplan code.

Please be aware that this code is case-sensitive and you will need to include the dashes within the passcode, but not when entering the ISBN. For further technical support, please visit www.MyKaplan.co.uk

Professional Examinations

Level 4

Personal Tax
(Finance Act 2013)

REVISION KIT

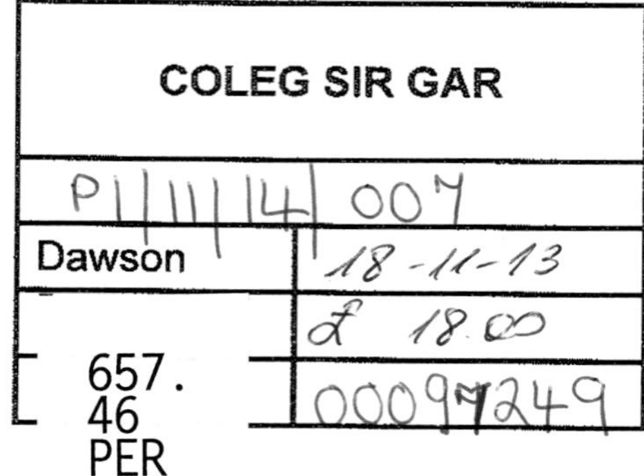

British Library Cataloguing-in-Publication Data

A catalogue record for this book is available from the British Library.

Published by:

Kaplan Publishing UK

Unit 2 The Business Centre

Molly Millar's Lane

Wokingham

Berkshire

RG41 2QZ

ISBN: 978-0-85732-906-6

Printed and bound in Great Britain.

Acknowledgements

We are grateful to HM Revenue and Customs for the provision of tax forms, which are Crown Copyright and are reproduced here with kind permission from the Office of Public Sector Information.

CONTENTS

Features in this exam kit

In addition to providing a wide ranging bank of real exam style questions, we have also included in this kit:

- Paper specific information and advice on exam technique.
- Our recommended approach to make your revision for this particular subject as effective as possible.

You will find a wealth of other resources to help you with your studies on the Kaplan and AAT websites:

www.mykaplan.co.uk

www.aat.org.uk/

INDEX TO QUESTIONS AND ANSWERS

PAPER ENHANCEMENTS

We have added the following enhancements to the answers in this exam kit:

Key answer tips

Some answers include key answer tips to help your understanding of each question.

Tutorial note

Some answers include tutorial notes to explain some of the technical points in more detail.

EXAM TECHNIQUE

- **Do not skip any of the material** in the syllabus.
- **Read each question** *very* carefully.
- **Double-check your answer** before committing yourself to it.
- Answer **every** question – if you do not know an answer to a multiple choice question or true/false question, you don't lose anything by guessing. Think carefully before you **guess.**
- If you are answering a multiple-choice question, **eliminate first those answers that you know are wrong**. Then choose the most appropriate answer from those that are left.
- **Don't panic** if you realise you've answered a question incorrectly. Getting one question wrong will not mean the difference between passing and failing

Computer-based exams – tips

- Do not attempt a CBT until you have **completed all study material** relating to it.
- On the AAT website there are practice CBTs. It is **ESSENTIAL** that you attempt at least one before your real CBT. You will become familiar with how to move around the CBT screens and the way that questions are formatted, increasing your confidence and speed in the actual exam.
- Be sure you understand how to use the **software** before you start the exam. If in doubt, ask the assessment centre staff to explain it to you.
- Questions are **displayed on the screen** and answers are entered using keyboard and mouse. At the end of the exam, you are given a certificate showing the result you have achieved unless some manual marking is required for the assessment.
- In addition to the traditional multiple-choice question type, CBTs will also contain **other types of questions**, such as number entry questions, drag and drop, true/false, pick lists or drop down menus or hybrids of these.
- In some CBTs you may have to type in complete computations or written answers.
- You need to be sure you **know how to answer questions** of this type before you sit the exam, through practice.

PAPER SPECIFIC INFORMATION

THE EXAM (AQ2013)

TIME ALLOWED

2 hours

DETAILED BREAKDOWN

The tasks in the assessment will always test the same areas as follows:

Task number	Topics	Maximum marks
1	Assessable benefits – provision of cars	9
2	Assessable benefits – all excluding cars	10
3	Income from property	10
4	Investment income	6
5	Computation of total and taxable income	12
6	Computation of tax payable and payment of tax	10
7	Theory underpinning topic and penalties	10
8	Tax returns	7
9	Basics of capital gains tax	12
10	Taxation of shares	8
11	Capital gains tax exemptions, losses, reliefs and tax payable	6

Task 7 will require a free text written response.

The chief assessor has stated that 'Students cannot avoid any of the key topics and to ensure success, must be prepared to answer written and computational style questions in any of the tasks.'

Note: The revision kit questions are grouped in the same order as the assessment.

PASS MARK

The pass mark for all AAT CBTs is 70%.

 **Always keep your eye on the clock and make sure you attempt all questions!**

DETAILED SYLLABUS

The detailed syllabus and study guide written by the AAT can be found at:

www.aat.org.uk/

THE EXAM (AQ2010)

The AQ2010 assessment covers the same syllabus as the AQ2013 assessment but has 23 tasks and is broken down into two sections which must both be passed in order to pass the assessment as a whole. In addition the individual tasks do not have mark allocations.

The time allowed and the pass mark are the same as the AQ2013 assessment.

The detailed breakdown of the AQ2010 assessment tasks is as follows. The relevant questions from the kit are shown alongside although some questions may cover more than one area.

Section 1		**Kit questions**
1.1	Legislation and procedures	66, 69, 71, 73, 75, 79 – 82
1.2	Duties and responsibilities of a tax practitioner	67, 68, 70, 72, 74
1.3	Legislative features of income from employment	76 – 78
1.4	Assessment for employment income	42 – 46
1.5	Assessable benefits – cars	1 – 5
1.6	Assessable benefits – all except cars	6 – 10, 16, 17
1.7	Exempt benefits	11 – 15
1.8	Deductions from employment income	47 – 51
1.9	Income from savings	These areas included in questions 30 -41
1.10	Income from dividends	
1.11	Exempt income	
1.12	Income tax computations	52 – 60
1.13	Self assessment and tax payments	61 – 65
1.14	Tax returns	83 – 86
Section 2		
2.1	Legislative features relating to property income	18, 19
2.2	Income from furnished and unfurnished property	20 – 24, 27, 28
2.3	Rent a room , furnished holiday accommodation	25, 26, 29
2.4	Chargeable assets, persons and disposals	87, 89, 91,
2.5	Capital gain computation	88 (a) (c), 90, 92, 93, 94(a), 108
2.6	Shares	100 – 104
2.7	Part disposals and chattels	88 (b), 94 (b), 95 – 98
2.8	Exempt assets, principal private residence	99, 108 (a) (b), 115 – 119
2.9	Annual exempt amount, loss relief and CGT payable	105 – 107, 108(c), 109, 111 – 114

Task 1.13 will normally require a free text written response.

EXAM GUIDANCE

- Some questions ask that answers be calculated to the nearest £. Some answers require students to calculate to the nearest £ and pence. If the question does not give any instructions then either method is acceptable and the computer will accept both.
- Some questions have scroll bars at the side. It is important that students scroll down and do not miss out parts of questions.
- Where free text written answers are required, students are supplied with a box to type their answers. This scrolls down as far as is necessary to accommodate the student answer.
- It is very important to read questions carefully. Common errors which have occurred in the assessments are:

  (i) Not spotting when salaries are given monthly and not annually

  (ii) Misreading dates

  (iii) Being unable to work out the number of months in a period when time apportionment is required. E.g. if a salary changes on 1 November then there are 7 months of the old salary and 5 of the new.
- Students often muddle up the contributions by employees when calculating car and fuel benefits.

KAPLAN'S RECOMMENDED REVISION APPROACH

QUESTION PRACTICE IS THE KEY TO SUCCESS

Success in professional examinations relies upon you acquiring a firm grasp of the required knowledge at the tuition phase. In order to be able to do the questions, knowledge is essential.

However, the difference between success and failure often hinges on your exam technique on the day and making the most of the revision phase of your studies.

The **Kaplan textbook** is the starting point, designed to provide the underpinning knowledge to tackle all questions. However, in the revision phase, poring over text books is not the answer.

The Kaplan workbook helps you consolidate your knowledge and understanding and is a useful tool to check whether you can remember key topic areas.

Kaplan pocket notes are designed to help you quickly revise a topic area, however you then need to practise questions. There is a need to progress to exam style questions as soon as possible, and to tie your exam technique and technical knowledge together.

The importance of question practice cannot be over-emphasised.

The recommended approach below is designed by expert tutors in the field, in conjunction with their knowledge of the examiner and the specimen assessment.

You need to practise as many questions as possible in the time you have left.

OUR AIM

Our aim is to get you to the stage where you can attempt exam questions confidently, to time, in a closed book environment, with no supplementary help (i.e. to simulate the real examination experience).

Practising your exam technique is also vitally important for you to assess your progress and identify areas of weakness that may need more attention in the final run up to the examination.

In order to achieve this we recognise that initially you may feel the need to practise some questions with open book help.

Good exam technique is vital.

THE KAPLAN PTAX REVISION PLAN

Stage 1: Assess areas of strengths and weaknesses

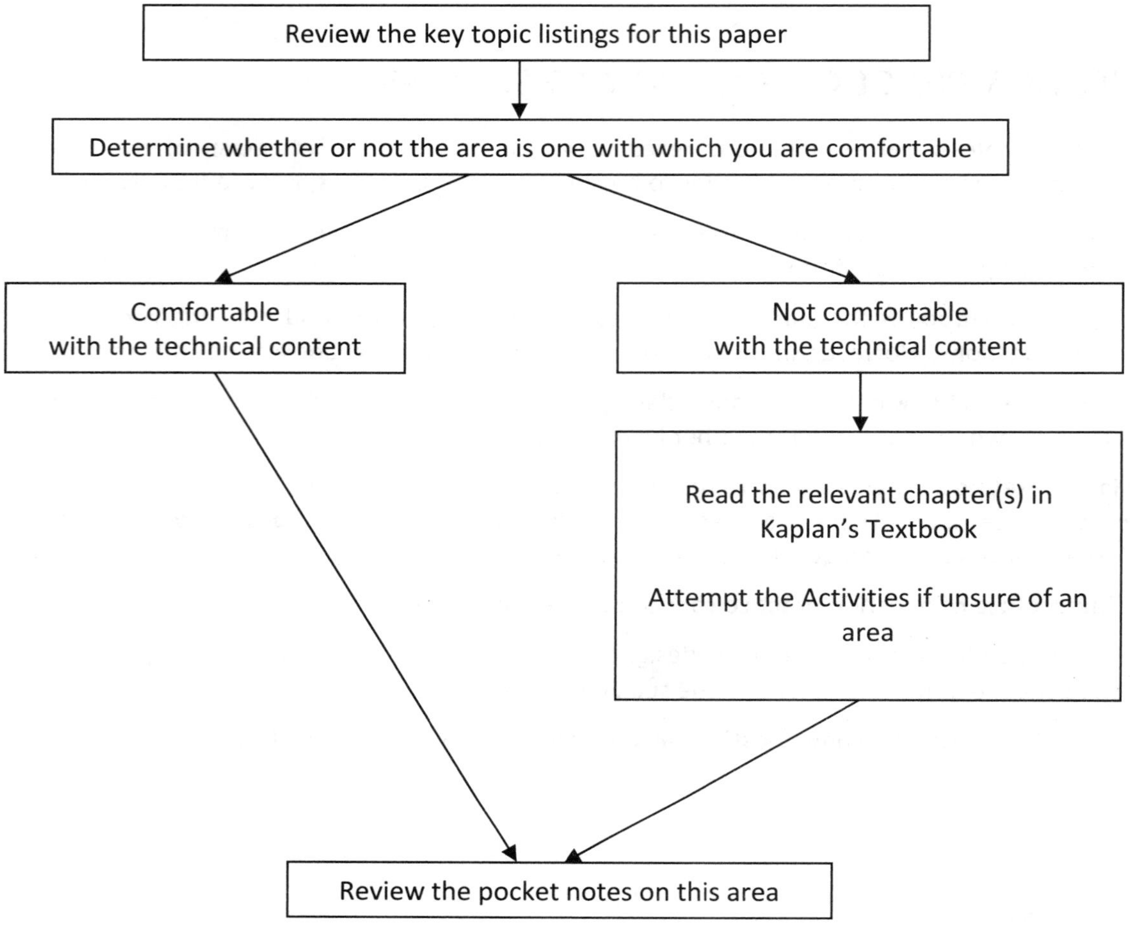

Stage 2: Practice questions

Follow the order of revision of topics as presented in this kit and attempt the questions in the order suggested.

Try to avoid referring to text books and notes and the model answer until you have completed your attempt.

Review your attempt with the model answer and assess how much of the answer you achieved.

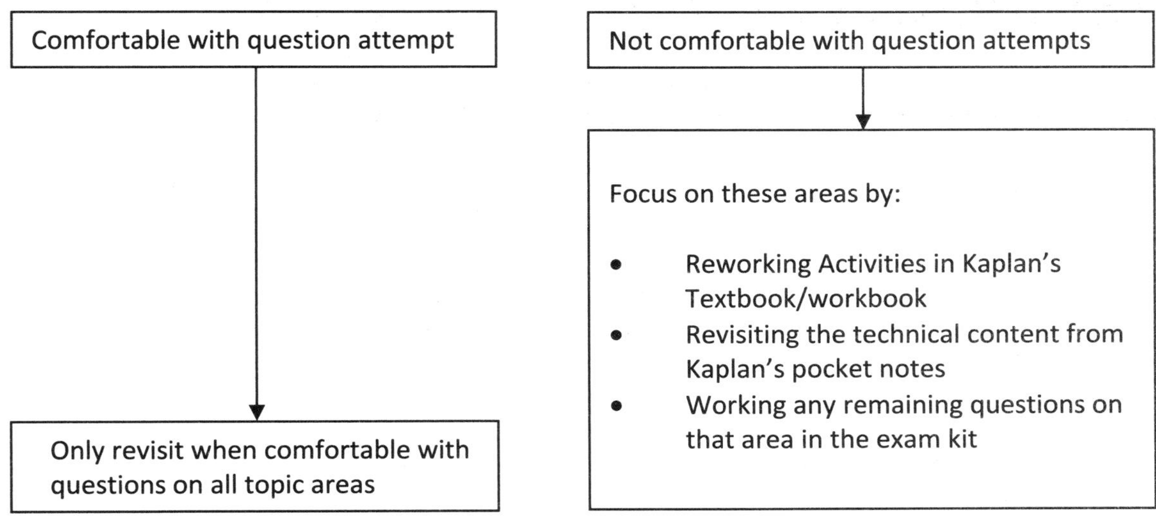

Stage 3: Final pre-exam revision

We recommend that you **attempt at least one two hour mock examination** containing a set of previously unseen exam standard questions.

Attempt the mock CBA online in timed, closed book conditions to simulate the real exam experience

You will find a mock CBA for this subject at www.mykaplan.co.uk

TAX RATES AND ALLOWANCES

Throughout this exam kit:

1. **You should assume that the tax rates and allowances for the tax year 2013/14 will continue to apply for the foreseeable future unless you are instructed otherwise.**
2. **Calculations and workings of tax liability should be made to the nearest penny.**
3. **All apportionments should be made to the nearest month.**

Tax rates and allowances similar to those below will be reproduced in the examination paper for Personal Tax.

In addition, other specific information necessary for candidates to answer individual questions will be given as part of the question.

Tax rates and bands

	%	
Basic rate	20	first £32,010
Higher rate	40	£32,011 to £150,000
Additional rate	45	over £150,000

Savings income is taxed at 10%, 20%, 40% and 45%.

(10% applies to a maximum of £2,790 of savings income only where non-savings income is below this limit)

Dividends are taxed at 10%, 32.5% and 37.5%.

Personal allowance

Personal allowance	Born after 5.4.1948	£9,440
Age allowance	Born between 6.4.1938 and 5.4.1948	£10,500
Age allowance	Born before 6.4.1938	£10,660
Income limit for age allowance		£26,100

Car benefit percentage

Emission rating	%
Zero	0
75 g/km or less	5
76 g/km to 94 g/km	10
95 g/km	11 + 1 for every extra 5 g/km above 95 g/km
Diesel engines	Additional 3%

The figure for fuel is £21,100.

Authorised mileage rates

First 10,000 miles	45p
Over 10,000 miles	25p

Van scale charge

Charge	£3,000
Private fuel provided	£564

Capital gains tax

Annual exempt amount	£10,900
Tax rate	18%
Higher rate	28%

HMRC official rate of interest	4.00%

TIME LIMITS AND ELECTION DATES

The following information is NOT given in the examination but is a useful summary for revision.

Capital gains tax

Determination of principal private residence	2 years from the acquisition of the second property	

Self assessment – individuals

Election / claim	Time limit	For 2013/14
Pay days for income tax and Class 4 NIC	1st instalment: 31 January in the tax year 2nd instalment: 31 July following the end of tax year Balancing payment: 31 Jan following the end of tax year	 31 January 2014 31 July 2014 31 January 2015
Pay day for CGT	31 January following the end of tax year	31 January 2015
Filing dates If return issued by 31 July in the tax year If return issued less than 3 months before the filing date	 Paper return: 31 October following end of tax year Electronic return: 31 January following end of tax year 3 months from the date of issue of the return	 31 October 2014 31 January 2015
Retention of records – Business records – Personal records	 5 years from 31 January following end of the tax year 12 months from 31 January following end of the tax year	 31 January 2020 31 January 2016
HMRC right of repair (i.e. to correct mistakes)	9 months from date the return was filed	
Taxpayers right to amend a return	12 months from 31 January following end of the tax year	31 January 2016
Recovery of overpaid tax	4 years following end of the tax year	5 April 2018
HMRC can open an enquiry	12 months from submission of the return	
Taxpayers right of appeal against an assessment	30 days from the assessment – appeal in writing	

PENALTIES

Offence		Penalty
Incorrect return	% of revenue lost (tax unpaid as a result of the error). Mistake Failure to take reasonable care Deliberate understatement Deliberate understatement with concealment Penalties can be reduced for taxpayer disclosure.	 Maximum % 0 30 70 100
Late notification	% of tax unpaid on 31 January following tax year end Percentages as for incorrect returns Penalties can be reduced for taxpayer disclosure.	
Late filing (cumulative)	Immediate penalty Delay 3–6 months Delay 6–12 months Delay of more than 12 months – no deliberate withholding of information – deliberate withholding of information – deliberate withholding of information with concealment	£100 £10 per day (max £900) 5% of tax due 5% of tax due Up to 70% tax due Up to 100% tax due
Late payment of tax (cumulative)	% of tax unpaid on 31 January following tax year end More than 30 days late More than 6 months late More than 12 months late	 5% of tax overdue 5% of tax overdue 5% of tax overdue
Failure to keep records		£3,000

Penalties can be reduced if the taxpayer has a **reasonable excuse.**

Section 1

PRACTICE QUESTIONS

INCOME TAX

ASSESSABLE BENEFITS – PROVISION OF CARS

Key answer tips

Task 1 in the AQ2013 assessment will cover this area and be worth a maximum of 9 marks.

1 SNAPE

Snape's employer gave him the choice of four company cars for 2013/14 with differing levels of CO_2 emissions. All the cars have petrol engines and the car would be provided from 6 April 2013.

(a) Calculate the scale percentage that will be applied for each car?

(i)	86 g/km	
(ii)	121 g/km	
(iii)	154 g/km	
(iv)	239 g/km	

(b) Snape chose a car with 154 g/km of emissions, but when it arrived it was a diesel engine car not petrol.

The car cost the employer £21,000 but this was with a discount of £995 from the original list price of £21,995.

The company pays for all running costs including the fuel although Hari contributes £50 per month towards private fuel.

(i)	What is the scale charge percentage for this car?	%
(ii)	What is the cost of the car to use in the assessable benefit calculation?	£
(iii)	What is the standard amount on which fuel benefit is calculated?	£
(iv)	What is Hari's fuel benefit?	£

2 SAM

(a) Which scale charge would be applied to calculate the assessable benefit for cars with the following CO_2 emissions?

Select ONE option for each answer.

(i) Petrol 93g/km

Options: 10%, 13%, 15%, 18%, 35%

(ii) Diesel 74 g/km

Options: 5%, 8%, 10%, 13%, 15%, 18%

(iii) Diesel 174 g/km

Options: 15%, 18%, 25%, 26%, 28%, 29%

(iv) Petrol 222 g/km

Options: 34%, 35%, 36%, 37%, 38%

(b) Sam was provided with a second hand company car in 2011.

When he received the car it had a market value of £17,000 but the car's list price when new was £27,000. The car has CO_2 emissions of 179 g/km and has a diesel engine.

In 2013/14 the company spent £750 on servicing and repairing the car, £620 on insurance and road tax and £2,000 on fuel for business trips.

Sam is not reimbursed for any of his private diesel costs.

(i) What is the scale charge percentage for this car?	%
(ii) What is the cost of the car to use in the assessable benefit calculation?	£
(iii) What is the amount of car running costs taxed on Sam in 2013/14?	£

3 FRODO

Frodo was provided with a petrol engine company car on 5 August 2013.

The car cost the company £24,000 but its list price was £26,000. The car has CO_2 emissions of 152 g/km. The company pays all running costs including fuel.

Frodo pays £100 per month to his employer which is £70 in respect of his private use of the car and £30 as a contribution towards his private fuel costs.

(a) What is the price used in calculating the car benefit?

A £24,000

B £26,000

(b) What is the scale charge % used to calculate the car benefit?

(c) What is Frodo's assessable car benefit for 2013/14?

(d) What is Frodo's assessable fuel benefit for 2013/14?

4 BARRY

(a) Barry was provided with a company car in January 2013.

The company paid the list price of £27,000 for the car but Barry contributed £6,000 to the company towards the purchase price. The car has a diesel engine and has CO_2 emissions of 174 g/km.

The company pays all the running costs of £1,650 per annum but does not pay any private fuel costs to Barry. Barry pays £50 per month to his employer for the private use of the car.

(i) What is the scale charge percentage for this car?

(ii) What is the cost of the car to use in the assessable benefit calculation?

(iii) What is Barry's assessable car benefit for 2013/14?

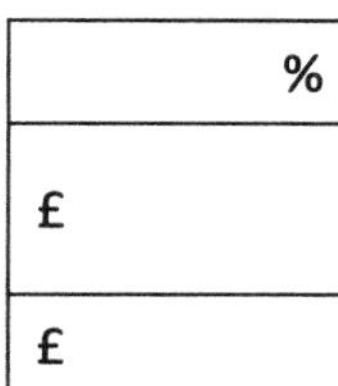

(b) Crouch has a company car with a list price of £20,000 which is taxed with a scale percentage of 24%. The car was first provided on 1 September 2013.

Crouch has all his private fuel paid for by the company although he reimburses the company 50% of the cost each month. The total private fuel cost (before deducting Crouch's contribution) is £2,920 for 2013/14.

What is Crouch's fuel benefit for 2013/14?

A £5,064

B £2,954

C £1,494

D £1,460

5 JACKIE

(a) Jackie is provided with a company car by her employer on 1 May 2013. The car has a diesel engine and has CO_2 emissions of 134 g/km. The car had a list price of £12,400.

The company had optional accessories costing £1,500 fitted to the car after it was delivered.

During 2013/14 the car was badly damaged in two accidents and Jackie was without the car for two weeks in August and another 3 weeks in October. She was not provided with a replacement car for these periods.

(i)	What is the scale charge percentage for this car?	%
(ii)	What is the cost of the car to use in the assessable benefit calculation?	£
(iii)	Jackie is not taxed on his car benefit for the 5 weeks during 2013/14 when the car is unavailable.	True/False
(iv)	What is Jackie's assessable car benefit for 2013/14?	

(b) Are the following statements true or false when determining that a car is to be treated as a pool car and give rise to no assessable benefit?

Tick the appropriate box for each statement.

	True	False
A pool car can be used exclusively by one employee		
A pool car is normally garaged at the company premises		
A pool car should only be used for business travel		

ASSESSABLE BENEFITS – ALL EXCLUDING CARS

Key answer tips

Task 2 in the AQ2013 assessment will cover this area and be worth a maximum of 10 marks. The task will usually have two or three parts. Some of the questions in this section of the kit are multi part but are not necessarily a 10 mark question. Others are shorter questions which give practice on the individual parts likely to be tested in this task.

6 BRIAN

(a) On 2 June 2013 Brian was provided by his employer with a laptop computer costing £750 for private use.

What is the assessable benefit for 2013/14?

(b) On 6 April 2013 Julie left her employment. She took up the offer of purchasing a camera for £200 which she had been lent by her employer several years previously.

This camera cost the company £500 and up to the end of 2012/13 Julie had been taxed on an assessable benefit totalling £350.

The camera was worth £250 at 6 April 2013.

What is Julie's assessable benefit for 2013/14?

(c) Which of the following situations would be treated as being job related where no accommodation benefit arises?

Assume that there are no special security considerations.

Tick the appropriate box for each option.

	Job related	Not job related
Accommodation provided for a lighthouse keeper		
Accommodation provided for executive directors		
Accommodation provided for non-executive directors		

(d) Since 1 August 2013, Esme has lived in a house provided by her employer.

This house cost her employers £175,000 in June 2006. The house has an annual value of £3,250 and Esme contributes £100 per month towards the cost of the benefit. The property had a market value of £228,000 when Esme moved in.

What is Esme's assessable benefit for 2013/14?

A £4,033

B £3,250

C £5,447

D £8,170

7 LOACH

(a) On 6 December 2013, Loach was provided with a company loan of £4,000 on which he pays interest at 2% per annum.

What is the taxable benefit for 2013/14?

A £53.33

B £Nil

C £26.67

D £80.00

(b) Swift plc purchased a property for £100,000 in December 2007. In May 2008 the company spent £30,500 on an extension to the property.

On 1 Nov 2012 an employee, Margarita, occupied the property. The market value of the property on 1 November 2012 was £220,000.

What is the additional 'expensive accommodation' benefit to be taxed on Margarita for 2013/14?

A £2,220

B £1,000

C £5,800

D £925

(c) Which of the following situations would be treated as being job related where no accommodation benefit arises?

Assume that there are no special security considerations.

Tick the appropriate box for each option.

	Job related	**Not job related**
Accommodation provided for a member of the clergy		
Accommodation provided for a zookeeper at Dudley Zoo		
Accommodation provided for directors to enable them to get to work more easily		

(d) Eve was provided with a flat (which was not job related) by her employer.

The flat has an annual value of £6,000 and Eve's employer pays rent of £450 per month. Eve pays £100 per month towards the private use of the flat.

What is Eve's taxable benefit for 2013/14?

A £5,400

B £6,000

C £4,800

D £4,200

(e) Read the following statements and tick the appropriate box to indicate whether they are true or false.

	True	False
Furniture provided by an employer is taxed at 25% of the market value per annum.		
Provision of workplace child care is an exempt benefit.		
Loans of up to £6,000 provided to employees in order that they can buy items wholly, exclusively and necessarily for their employment are exempt from income tax		
Reimbursement of expenses for home to work travel is tax allowable for the employee.		

8 BHARAT

(a) On 6 October 2013, Bharat was provided with a home cinema system worth £3,600 by his employer. The cinema system is only used for private purposes.

What is the assessable benefit for 2013/14?

A £720

B £360

C £420

D £Nil

(b) When accommodation is purchased by an employer for use by an employee, what is the value of the property above which an additional benefit is applied?

A £80,000

B £75,000

C £85,000

D £125,000

(c) Which of the following situations would be treated as being job related where no accommodation benefit arises?

Assume that there are no special security considerations.

Tick the appropriate box for each option.

	Job related	**Not job related**
Accommodation provided for a school caretaker		
Accommodation provided for the Prime Minister		
Accommodation provided for a sales director so that he may entertain prospective customers		

(d) Sybil was provided with a flat (which is not job related) by her employer.

The flat has an annual value of £5,600 and Sybil's employer pays rent of £420 per month. Sybil pays £80 per month towards the private use of the flat.

What is Sybil's taxable benefit for 2013/14?

(e) Which of the following statements are correct for accommodation which is not job related?

(i) Furniture provided by an employer is an exempt benefit

(ii) Furniture provided by an employer is taxed on the cost to the employer in the year of purchase

(iii) Accommodation expenses paid for by the employer are taxed on the cost to the employer

(iv) If the employer provides furniture with accommodation it is an additional benefit to the employee

A (ii) and (iii)

B (i) and (iii)

C (iii) and (iv)

D (iv) only

9 NIKITA

(a) On 6 October 2013, Nikita was provided with a company loan of £28,000 on which she pays interest at 1% per annum. The official rate of interest is 4.00%.

What is the assessable benefit for 2013/14?

(b) Percy's employer provides him with a van for private use. The van has a market value of £20,000. Percy has the use of the van throughout 2013/14.

What is the assessable benefit for 2013/14?

A £4,000

B £3,000

C £2,000

D £5,000

(c) Are the following benefits assessable on P11D employees only or all employees?

Tick the appropriate box for each option.

	P11D employee	**All employees**
Cash vouchers		
Additional benefit for accommodation costing over a certain limit		
Cars		

(d) Molly earns £20,000 per year and was provided with a house (which is not job related) by her employer.

The house has an annual value of £5,000 and cost Molly's employer £150,000 in September 2012. The house contains furniture costing £40,000. Heating bills of £750 per year are paid by her employer. Molly pays £200 per month towards the private use of the house.

What is Molly's taxable benefit for 2013/14?

(e) Which two of the following statements are correct?

(i) Assets lent to an employee are taxed at 20% of the market value per annum.

(ii) Assets lent to an employee are taxed at 4.00% of the market value per annum.

(iii) The car benefit for a pool car is limited to 10% of the total benefit.

(iv) Loan benefits can be reduced by any payments made by the employee.

A (i) and (iii)

B (ii) and (iii)

C (iii) and (iv)

D (i) and (iv)

10 GIBBS

(a) Gibbs is provided with accommodation by his employers, Tallmark plc.

The property cost Tallmark plc £250,000 in May 2010 and the company spent £45,000 on improvements in June 2013.

The property has an annual value of £6,500 and Gibbs pays rent of £150 per month to Hallmark plc. The property had a market value of £265,000 when Gibbs moved in on 20 December 2010.

What is the assessable benefit in 2013/14 for the provision of the accommodation?

A £14,100

B £12,300

C £13,500

D £11,700

(b) Ducky is provided with a house by his employers.

The property was furnished by his employers at a cost of £20,000. They also paid for regular gardening and cleaning at the property which cost them a total of £2,100 for 2013/14. In addition they spent £5,600 during 2013/14 on installing new double glazed windows.

What is the assessable benefit for the furniture and the expenses incurred?

(c) Betsy earns £6,400 per year. During 2013/14 she receives a £100 payment under her employer's staff suggestion scheme in respect of a proposal she made that reduced the costs incurred by the business.

Her employer also pays her home telephone bills of £400 even though Betsy has no business use of the telephone.

What is Betsy's total assessable benefit in respect of the payment under the staff suggestion scheme and the telephone bills?

(d) Betsy's employers move to larger premises which have a staff canteen available to all staff.

Betsy is entitled to subsidised meals in the canteen and pays £1 per day. The free meals cost her employer £480 per year to provide for 250 days.

What is Betsy's assessable benefit in respect of the canteen?

A £480

B £230

C £Nil

D £96

11 EXEMPT BENEFITS

The following sentences all relate to exempt/partly exempt benefits provided to P11D employees.

Complete the sentences correctly using one of the options provided.

(a) Interest free loans made by an employer to an employee are exempt provided the total of loans provided during the tax year does not exceed £................

Options: £1,000, £3,000, £5,000, £7,000

(b) An employer can pay home workers additional household expenses of up to £.............. per week tax free, without the need for the employee to provide supporting evidence.

Options: £2, £3, £4, £5

(c) Approved childcare payments to employees paying tax at the additional rate are tax free up to £................per week.

Options: £22, £25, £28, £45, £55

12 PERDITA

Perdita has asked you to advise her of which of the following benefits, provided to employees earning £18,000 per year, are exempt.

Tick one box on each line.

	Exempt	Not exempt
One mobile telephone per employee		
Use of a pool car		
Use of a van for a fortnight's camping holiday. There is no other private use.		
Provision of a car parking space in a multi-storey car park near the place of work		
Childcare vouchers of £50 per week spent with an unapproved child minder		
Provision of bicycles for staff who have worked for the company for at least seven years		
Provision of an interest free loan of £4,000 made on 6 April 2013 and written off on 5 April 2014: – provision of loan – write off of loan		

13 JOEY

The following sentences all relate to benefits. Complete the sentences correctly using one of the options provided.

(a) In order for Joey, who is not a director, to be classed as a P11D employee he must earn at least £................ per annum.

Options: £5,000, £7,500, £8,500, £10,500

(b) The assessable benefit for a pool car with CO_2 emissions of 137 g/km and a list price of £15,000 which runs on petrol is £..............................

Options: £0, £2,700, £2,850, £3,000

(c) The maximum capital contribution that can be deducted from the list price when calculating a car benefit is £...........................

Options: £1,000, £3,000, £5,000, £7,000

14 HAYLEY

Complete the following sentences so that the benefit is exempt from tax.

(a) Personal expenses paid to Hayley whilst working away in the UK are exempt up to £......... per night.

Options: £6; £5; £4; £3; £2

(b) Exempt payments towards staff entertainment are restricted to £.......... per employee.

Options: £100; £125; £150; £175

(c) Relocation expenses up to £............... are an exempt benefit.

Options: £5,000; £6,000; £7,000; £8,000

15 HF LTD

(a) HF Ltd is considering whether to provide its employees with fitness facilities.

They have to decide between the following options:

(i) Building a gym at the company premises which will only be open to employees. The annual running costs of the gym would be £450 per employee.

(ii) Paying annual subscriptions at health clubs and gyms near to the employees' homes. Subscriptions up to £450 would be paid for each employee.

Which of these options results in a lower assessable benefit for individual employees?

A (i)

B (ii)

C Neither, because they both produce the same result.

(b) Long service awards up to £..................... per year of service are tax free.

Options: £25; £50; £75; £100

(c) Long service awards for .... years or more of service are tax free.

Options: 10; 15; 20; 25

(d) A long service award will only be exempt provided no similar payment has been made within the last ....years

Options: 5; 10; 15; 20

16 JADEJA PLC

Jadeja plc provides the following benefits to employees earning at least £10,000 per year. Which of them are exempt, partly exempt or taxable for the recipient?

Tick one box on each line.

	Exempt	Not exempt	Partly exempt
Free annual health screening which costs the employer £350 per head.			
An annual staff party which costs £220 per head			
Payments of £7 per night for personal expenses when employees have to stay away from home elsewhere in the UK			
Removal expenses of £12,000 paid to an employee who had to relocate to a new town when she was promoted			
Childcare vouchers of £40 per week provided to employees earning between £50,000 and £100,000 per year			
A smart phone issued to all staff of manager grade			

17 DHONI LTD

Which of the following benefits provided to employees of Dhoni Ltd earning at least £12,000 per year are exempt or taxable, for the recipient?

Tick one box on each line.

	Exempt	Taxable
Payment of £800 fees for office employees attending computer skills courses		
Free tickets for all staff to attend a high profile athletics event sponsored by the employer. The tickets cost members of the public £25.		
Long service awards of £500 cash for employees completing 20 years service		
Private medical insurance for employees who work only in the UK		
A payment of £500 to an employee in accordance with the rules of the staff suggestion scheme.		
Free eye tests for all staff working with computers		

INCOME FROM PROPERTY

Key answer tips

Task 3 in the AQ2013 assessment will cover this area and be worth a maximum of 10 marks. The task will usually have two or three parts. Some of the questions in this section of the kit are multi part but are not necessarily a 10 mark question. Others are shorter questions which give practice on the individual parts likely to be tested in this task.

18 GED

Are the following statements true or false?

Tick one box on each line.

	TRUE	FALSE
Property losses from furnished lettings cannot be deducted from profits on unfurnished lettings.		
Ged and his wife occupy the same property. They can each have a rent a room exemption of £4,250.		
Income from property is taxed on an accruals basis.		
Broad receives a salary of £25,000 and £3,000 rent from letting out a room in his house. He has no other rental income. He will not have to pay any tax on the rent.		

19 HOWARD

Which of the following expenses would not be deductible by Howard from rental income in respect of an unfurnished flat?

(i) Water rates

(ii) Wear and tear allowance

(iii) Installation of a new central heating boiler

(iv) Advertising for a new tenant

A (i) and (ii)

B (ii), (iii) and (iv)

C (i) and (iv)

D (ii) and (iii)

20 GEORGIA

Georgia has two properties, details of which are:

One bedroom flat:

1 This furnished flat has been occupied by the same tenants for several years, and the rent was £500 per month during 2013, payable on the first of the month. On 1 January 2014 the rent was increased to £525 per month, still payable on the first day of each month.

2 Georgia incurred insurance of £200 in respect of 2013/14. She also paid for various repairs totalling £850 which included £500 for the cost of a new boiler.

Four bedroom house:

3 This unfurnished house is rented out for £480 per month, but was empty until 1 November 2013 when a family moved in on a twelve month lease.

4 Georgia paid for a gardener to maintain the large garden at a cost of £20 per month from 1 November 2013.

Calculate the profit or loss made on each property using the following table.

	One bedroom flat £	*Four bedroom house* £
Income:		
Expenses:		

21 SHEILA

Sheila has two properties, details of which are:

Three bedroom house:

1 This unfurnished house is rented out for £1,000 per month. The property was occupied until 1 September 2013 when the tenants suddenly moved out, owing the rent for August. Sheila knows she will not recover this rent. The property was let again from 1 December 2013 to another family.

2 The only expense paid by Sheila in respect of the house was 5% commission to the agent on rent received.

Two bedroom flat:

3 This furnished flat is rented out for £600 per month. The property was occupied by Sheila during April 2013. It was then unoccupied until 1 July when a couple moved in on a twelve month lease.

4 Sheila incurred council tax and water rates on the flat, totalling £1,250 for 2013/14. She also paid insurance of £400.

Calculate the profit or loss made on each property using the following table.

	Three bedroom house £	*Two bedroom flat* £
Income:		
Expenses:		

22 WILL

Will has three properties, details of which are:

Two bedroom cottage:

1 This furnished cottage is rented out for £500 per month.

2 Will pays gardeners fees of £50 a month and cleaners bills of £70 a month. He also paid for repairs costing £400.

One bedroom flat:

3 This furnished flat is rented out for £3,600 per year. The property was unoccupied until 6 July 2013.

4 Will paid water rates of £500 and insurance of £500 in respect of the flat.

Three bedroom house:

5 This unfurnished house is rented for £4,300 a year.

6 Will paid insurance of £1,000 for the year ended 30 September 2013. This went up to £1,200 for the year ended 30 September 2014.

Calculate the profit or loss made on each property using the following table.

	Two bedroom cottage £	*One bedroom flat* £	*Three bedroom house* £
Income:			
Expenses:			

23 EDWARD

Edward has two properties, details of which are:

Four bedroom house:

1 This unfurnished house is rented out for £7,200 per annum. The property was occupied until 31 January 2014 when the tenants suddenly moved out, without paying the rent for January. The property was let again from 1 May 2014 to another family.

2 The only expenses paid by Edward in respect of the house were £500 for gardening and £1,200 on fitting a new kitchen

Two bedroom bungalow:

3 This furnished bungalow is rented out for £550 per month. The property was unoccupied until 6 October 2013.

4 Edward paid council tax bills of £1,100 for the bungalow in respect of 2013/14. He also paid for repairs to the property costing £150.

Calculate the profit or loss made on each property using the following table.

	Four bedroom house £	*Two bedroom bungalow* £
Income		
Expenses:		

24 REBECCA

Rebecca owns three properties: 15 Olden Way, 29 Harrow Crescent and 42 Long Close. All three properties are let on a furnished basis.

1 15 Olden Way: this property was bought in December 2008.

The rent is £600 per month and the property was occupied throughout the whole of 2013/14.

In May 2013 Rebecca purchased furniture at a cost of £2,100.

2 29 Harrow Crescent: this property was bought in June 2010.

The rent is £500 per month. The property was occupied until 30 June 2013 when the tenants moved out. The new tenants moved in on 1 January 2014.

3 42 Long Close: this property was bought on 1 August 2013.

When Rebecca bought the property it was unfurnished, so she spent £3,000 on furniture before the first tenants moved in on 1 November 2013.

The monthly rental is £750.

Expenses for the three properties are:

	15 Olden Way	*29 Harrow Crescent*	*42 Long Close*
	£	£	£
Insurance:			
12 months to 31 December 2013	150	120	
12 months to 31 December 2014	180	140	
12 months to 31 July 2014			160
Water rates – all allowable	80	100	85

Calculate the profit or loss made on each property using the following table.

	15 Olden Way £	*29 Harrow Crescent* £	*42 Long Close* £
Income			
Expenses:			

25 WINSTON

Winston is thinking about renting out a room in his house.

He asks you the following questions.

(a) How much rent can he receive from his lodger free of tax under the rent a room scheme?

£......................................

(b) Does the rent a room limit apply to the rents net of expenses? Yes/No

(c) If he takes in two lodgers will he get a separate rent a room relief for each of them? Yes/No

(d) If he lets a room unfurnished will the rent a room relief still apply? Yes/No

26 BOB

(a) Bob rents out a furnished room in his main residence for £70 per week throughout 2013/14. He incurs expenses of £2,000.

What is his assessable property income? £............................

(b) Barry rents out the furnished attic room of his 4 bedroom house for £2,000 per month. He incurs property expenses of £300 per month.

What is his assessable property income? £............................

(c) Where a lodger pays rent in excess of the rent a room limit, the landlord must make a claim to HMRC if he wishes to apply rent a room relief. True/False

27 WEAR AND TEAR ALLOWANCE

(a) Which two of the following statements are true?

A Wear and tear allowance is deductible for all rental properties

B When calculating wear and tear allowance, council tax only must be deducted

C When calculating wear and tear allowance, all expenses paid by the landlord which are normally the responsibility of the tenant must be deducted

D When calculating wear and tear allowance, only rents received net of bad debts are included

(b) True or false:

Property losses can be offset against an individual's total income in the tax year.

(c) True or false:

When calculating an individual's property income any costs of improving the property are not allowable.

28 ROSALIE

(a) Rosalie rents out a house. In the year ended 30 June 2013 she paid insurance of £1,800 and in the year ended 30 June 2014 £2,160.

What is her allowable expense against her property income?

Options: £1,800, £2,160, £2,070, £1,890, £2,040

(b) Which one of the following statements is incorrect?

A Wear and tear allowance is reduced if the landlord pays water rates

B A landlord can deduct capital expenditure from his property income

C Any bad debts incurred are allowable expenditure when calculating property income

D Individuals calculate their property income for the tax year

(c) True or false:

Losses made on renting out a property can only be offset against property profits.

(d) True or false:

Any property losses which cannot be offset in the year they are incurred cannot be carried forward.

29 LAURIE

As well as his own private residence, Laurie owns a country cottage which he uses for holidays. He is thinking of renting this property out for short holiday lets of one or two weeks each during the Summer holiday season. He asks you the following questions.

Tick the appropriate column for each question.

	Yes	**No**
Can I use the rent a room exemption for letting my country cottage?		
If I let the property out for 17 weeks out of the 35 weeks it is available, can I claim to treat it as a furnished holiday letting?		
If the cottage is classed as furnished holiday accommodation and the letting makes a loss, do I have to carry the loss forward against future rental profits in respect of furnished holiday accommodation?		

INVESTMENT INCOME

Key answer tips

Task 4 in the AQ2013 assessment will cover this area and be worth a maximum of 6 marks. The task may have several parts. Some of the questions in this section of the kit are multi part but are not necessarily a 6 mark question. Others are shorter questions which give practice on the individual parts likely to be tested in this task.

30 PATRICIA

(a) During 2013/14 Patricia received interest of £320 from her ISA and £480 from her NS&I bank account.

How much tax has been deducted from this interest?

(b) Place the following types of investment income received by an individual in the appropriate column in the table below.

- Interest on 3½% War Loan (a government stock)
- Bank deposit interest
- Building society interest
- Interest on unquoted loan notes in a UK company
- Interest from NS&I bank accounts

Received gross	**Received net**

(c) Ian receives a dividend of £326 in May 2013. He has taxable income, including the dividend, of £60,000.

What is the additional tax due from Ian on his dividend?

A £117.72

B £81.50

C £36.22

D £0

(d) Is the following statement true or is it false?

Griffith is 55. His only income is dividends of £25,000 (gross amount).

He will be entitled to a tax repayment of £944.

31 RAVI

(a) Ravi is aged 45. Complete the following sentence.

The maximum amount that Ravi can invest in an ISA during 2013/14 is £..................

(b) Is the following statement true or is it false?

Gambling winnings are always exempt from income tax no matter how large the sum received.

(c) Joe is aged 68. His only income is building society interest of £11,000 which he has received gross. What is his tax payable? £..........................

32 HANNAH

(a) Which two of the following types of income are exempt from income tax?

- National lottery winnings
- Property income
- NS&I bank interest
- NS&I Savings Certificate interest

(b) During 2013/14, Hannah received interest of £860 from her bank account and £480 from a cash ISA.

What is the gross interest to be included in her taxable income calculation?

A £860

B £1,555

C £1,075

D £1,675

33 CASTILAS

(a) Castilas is 55. His only income for 2013/14 is a dividend of £12,000 (gross amount).

How will the excess of this dividend income over his personal allowance be taxed (before considering tax credits)?

A The first £2,790 at 10% and the rest at 20%

B All at 10%

C All at 20%

D Partly at 10% and partly at 32.5%

(b) What tax repayment will Castilas receive for 2013/14?

A £944.00

B £1,200.00

C £256.00

D £Nil

34 JAL

(a) Place the following types of investment income in the appropriate column in the table below.

- Interest on Treasury Stock (a government stock)
- Interest on ISAs
- Interest on Sketch Ltd unquoted loan notes
- Interest on a building society account
- Interest on NS&I Savings Certificates
- Premium bond winnings

Received net	Received gross	Exempt

(b) During 2013/14, Jal received interest of £120 from her building society account and £160 from her Maxxie Ltd unquoted debentures.

The tax credits related to this interest totals:

A £70

B £30

C £40

D £56

35 NAOMI

(a) Naomi receives a dividend of £280 in May 2013.

What is the tax credit attached to this dividend?

(b) What is the gross amount of the dividend to include in Naomi's tax computation?

36 THERESE

Mark the following statements as true or false.

	True	False
If Therese has winnings from Premium Bonds they must be declared on her tax return.		
If the tax liability of an individual who has dividend income only is less than the tax credit on the dividend, then a repayment can be claimed.		

37 KIRA

Kira has received cash from the following sources.

For each source tick Yes if it is chargeable to income tax and tick No if it is not.

	Yes	No
Profit on disposal of an asset		
Rental profits		
Tips earned whilst working in a bar		
Damages for injury at work		

38 GINNY

(a) Place the following types of investment income in the appropriate column in the table below:

- Interest from National Savings Certificates
- Interest from building society accounts
- Interest from bank accounts
- Interest from Individual Savings Accounts
- NS&I bank Interest
- Interest from Gilts (Government stocks)

Exempt from income tax	Taxable

(b) During 2013/14, Ginny received interest of £160 from her quoted loan notes in Potter plc and £360 from her bank account.

What is the gross taxable amount of interest?

A £578

B £560

C £610

D £650

(c) Hermione receives a dividend of £243 in December 2013.

What is the tax credit attached to this dividend? £..................................

What is the gross amount of the dividend? £..................................

39 TARAN

(a) Complete the following sentence.

In 2013/14 the maximum amount that Taran (aged 42) can invest in a cash ISA is £……………………

(b) Is the following statement true?

Dividends received from an ISA are always exempt from tax.

(c) Is the following statement true?

When shares held in an ISA are sold, the capital gain is exempt.

40 LANG

Lang has received £340 interest from the Blankshire Building society and £140 interest on an NS&I investment account.

Which of the following statements are incorrect?

(i) Interest from the Blankshire Building society is paid net of 20% tax.

(ii) The first £100 of NS&I bank account interest is exempt income.

(iii) If this interest was Lang's only income, he would be entitled to a tax repayment of £68.

A (ii) only

B (ii) and (iii)

C All of them

D (i) and (iii)

41 HUANG

Huang is 40 years old. He receives dividends of £10,800 from an investment company plus £1,800 of dividends from shares held in his ISA account.

What is his income tax liability?

A £256.00

B £1,200.00

C £1,400.00

D £Nil

COMPUTATION OF TOTAL AND TAXABLE INCOME

Key answer tips

Task 5 in the AQ2013 assessment will cover this area and be worth a maximum of 12 marks. The task will usually have two or three parts. Some of the questions in this section of the kit are multi part but are not necessarily a 12 mark question. Others are shorter questions which give practice on the individual parts likely to be tested in this task.

42 JESSICA

Jessica provides you with the following information:

(i) Her annual salary for the twelve months to 30 April 2013 was £36,300.

(ii) Her annual salary for the twelve months to 30 April 2014 was £20,000.

(iii) She received a bonus of £2,300 on 1 May 2013 based on the company's accounting profit for the year ended 30 April 2013.

(iv) She received a bonus of £1,300 on 1 May 2014 based on the company's accounting profit for the year ended 30 April 2014.

(v) She receives commission of 7.5% of her salary each month.

Using this information, answer the following questions.

Select one of the options given after each question.

(a) What is the salary taxable for 2013/14?

Options: £20,000; £21,358; £22,716; £34,942; £36,300

(b) What is the bonus taxable for 2013/14?

Options: £1,300; £2,216; £2,300; £3,600

(c) What is the commission taxable for 2013/14?

Options: £1,500; £1,602; £2,722; £2,620

43 JANE

Jane is employed by Berrow plc. For the year ended 30 June 2013 she received an annual salary of £18,000 and for the year ended 30 June 2014 her salary was increased to £20,000. Jane received her salary in equal monthly instalments.

The company pays out bonuses each year which are related to the level of profits in the year ended 30 June. Jane received her bonus of £1,000 for the year ended 30 June 2012 on 14 April 2013. She received £1,050 for the year ended 30 June 2013 which was paid on 17 April 2014.

She also received a commission each year equal to 6% of her annual salary. This was paid monthly together with her salary.

Using this information, calculate the correct answers to questions (a) and (b) and (c).

(a) What is the salary taxable for 2013/14?

(b) What is the bonus taxable in 2013/14?

(c) Calculate the commission taxable in 2013/14.

44 EFFIE

Effie provides you with the following information.

(i) Her annual salary for the 12 months to 30 September 2013 was £30,000.

(ii) Her annual salary for the 12 months to 30 September 2014 was £33,600.

Her salary is paid in equal monthly instalments.

(iii) Effie pays an annual contribution of £480 to a registered charity through the payroll giving scheme.

(iv) Effie also makes a payment of £800 to her local church (also a registered charity) through the Gift Aid scheme.

(v) She receives reimbursed employment expenses of £1,260 during 2013/14. Her employer has a dispensation from HMRC in respect of these expenses.

What is her taxable employment income for 2013/14?

A £31,800

B £31,320

C £32,580

D £30,320

45 HARRY

Harry provides you with the following information.

His monthly salary was £1,300 until 31 December 2013. From 1 January 2014 he received a monthly salary of £1,600.

Harry also receives an annual bonus based on profits which is paid to him on 15 April following the company's year end of 31 December. His bonus for the year ended 31 December 2012 was £1,125, for the year ended 31 December 2013 was £1,200 and for the year ended 31 December 2014 was £1,500.

Using this information, answer the following questions.

Select one of the options given after each question.

(a) What is Harry's taxable salary for 2013/14?

Options: £15,600, £19,200, £16,500, £16,800, £18,300

(b) What is Harry's taxable bonus for 2013/14?

Options: £1,125, £1,200, £1,500, £1,144, £1,275

46 MANINDER

Maninder has given you the following details about her employment income.

(i) She receives a salary of £25,000 per year.

(ii) She pays a donation to charity each month of £20 through the payroll giving scheme.

(iii) She contributes 5% of her salary to her employer's occupational pension scheme.

(iv) She receives a round sum allowance of £1,000 per month of which 70% is spent on business travel and subsistence and 30% on entertaining clients.

What is Maninder's assessable employment income?

A £23,510

B £23,750

C £27,110

D £35,510

47 SALLY

(a) Sally uses her own car for business travel.

During 2013/14 she travelled 20,000 business miles for which she was paid 25p per mile by her employer.

The impact of this is:

A She will have taxable employment income of £2,000

B She will have taxable employment income of £4,000

C She will claim an allowable expense of £2,000

D She will claim an allowable expense of £4,000

(b) Ruth is a member of an occupational pension scheme to which she contributes 5% of her salary. Her employer also makes a contribution equal to 5% of her salary.

For 2013/14 her salary was £45,000.

Which ONE of the following statements is correct?

A Her contribution is £2,250 which is a tax allowable deduction from her gross salary

B Both the employee's and employer's contributions are tax allowable deductions from her gross salary

C Her income tax payable will be reduced by £2,250

D Her income tax payable will be reduced by £4,500

(c) Tilly receives a round sum allowance of £5,000 per annum.

Out of this allowance she pays £800 for business travel and £150 for professional subscriptions. The rest is used for client entertaining.

Which ONE of the following statements is correct?

A She will be taxed on the full £5,000 allowance with no deductions

B She will be taxed on a net sum of £4,850

C She will be taxed on a net sum of £4,050

D She will not be taxed on any of the round sum allowance

(d) Henry is an employee. He has a personal pension scheme.

Which ONE of the following statements is **always** true?

A Henry's employer does not have an occupational pension scheme

B Henry's employer does have an occupational pension scheme but Henry is not allowed to join it

C Henry can contribute into his personal pension scheme and into his employer's occupational pension scheme (if there is one) and receive tax relief for both contributions provided his total contributions do not exceed certain limits

D Henry's employer must pay contributions to Henry's personal pension scheme

48 BERNIE

Read the following statements about pension contributions and tick the relevant box to mark each one as true or false.

	True	False
Bernie cannot contribute to both a personal pension scheme and to his employer's occupational scheme.		
Personal pension scheme payments are made net of 10% tax.		
Relief for occupational pension payments is given by deducting the payments made from gross earnings.		
Gary pays a cheque for £260 to his personal pension scheme. He will obtain tax relief by extending his basic rate band by £260.		
Sobia is currently unemployed and has no earnings. She cannot contribute to a personal pension scheme because she has no relevant earnings.		
Pension contributions made by an employer on behalf of an employee are an assessable benefit.		

49 MICHELLE

Read the following statements about expense payments and tick the relevant box to mark each one as true or false.

	True	False
Michelle is employed as a tax consultant. She pays £520 per annum in subscriptions. £380 is paid to the Chartered Institute of Taxation and £140 to a local health club where Michelle often meets clients. Both subscriptions can be deducted from her employment income for tax purposes.		
In order for employment expenses to be deductible from employment income, they must be incurred wholly, exclusively and naturally in the performance of the employment.		
An employee spends £35 on taking a client out for lunch. His employer reimburses him for this amount. The employee will not be taxed on the £35 received.		
Sam is an accountancy trainee employed by a firm of accountants. He has to travel 10 miles per day to get to and from his place of employment. He can claim the costs of travelling as a deduction from his employment income for tax purposes.		
Cook pays £10 per month to Oxfam (an international charity) through the payroll giving scheme. This is a tax allowable deduction from his gross salary.		

50 RON

(a) Ron uses his own car for business travelling.

During 2013/14 he travelled 18,000 business miles for which he was paid 38p per mile by his employer.

What is the tax impact of this?

A He will claim a tax allowable expense of £340

B He will claim a tax allowable expense of £1,260

C He will have a taxable amount of £340

D He will have a taxable amount of £1,260

(b) George has made £400 of donations in 2013/14.

£150 was paid to a registered charity through the payroll giving scheme and the other £250 was paid to a political party.

Can either of these donations be deducted from employment income for tax purposes?

A Both are allowable as a deduction

B Neither of them is allowed as a deduction

C Only the political donation is allowable

D Only the charitable donation is allowable

(c) Fred has an occupational pension scheme to which he contributes 7% of his salary whilst his employer contributes 3%.

For 2013/14 his salary was £31,000.

The impact of this is:

A His basic rate band will be extended by £2,170

B He can deduct £2,170 from his salary as a tax allowable amount

C His basic rate band will be extended by £3,100

D He can deduct £3,100 from his salary as a tax allowable amount

(d) Complete the following by selecting one option for each blank.

An individual can obtain tax relief on personal pension contributions on the higher of

(i) £............................gross or

Options: £3,400, £3,600, £3,800, £4,000

(ii) ....% of relevant earnings

Options: 15%, 35%, 50%, 75%, 100%

51 ASIF

(a) Asif has made £600 of donations in 2013/14.

£120 was paid to a registered charity through the Gift Aid scheme and the other £480 was paid to a charity through the payroll giving scheme.

Can either of these donations be deducted from employment income for tax purposes?

A Both are allowable as a deduction

B Neither of them is allowed as a deduction

C Only the payroll giving donation is allowable

D Only the Gift Aid donation is allowable

(b) Which of the following statements about pension contributions are incorrect?

(i) Personal pension contributions are paid net of 20% tax relief.

(ii) Personal pension contributions reduce taxable income.

(iii) Personal pension contributions can be made by both employed and self employed individuals.

(iv) Non-contributory occupational pension schemes do not require the taxpayer to make any contributions.

(v) A taxpayer with earnings of £10,000 can make personal pension contributions up to a maximum of £3,600.

A (i) and (ii)

B (ii) and (iv)

C (iii) and (iv)

D (ii) and (v)

E (iv) and (v)

(c) Asif has used his own car for business travel.

In 2013/14 he travelled 20,000 miles of which 6,000 were for home to work travel. His employer has paid him 28p per mile for the 20,000 miles.

The impact of this is:

A He will have a tax allowable expense of £100

B He will have a taxable amount of £100

C He will have a tax allowable expense of £1,400

D He will have a taxable amount of £1,400

52 ARKAN

Arkan, who is aged 46, gives you the following information about his income tax for 2013/14.

(1) His annual salary was £90,000 until 1 October 2013 when he received a 3% pay rise.

(2) He has the use of a company car for which the annual assessable benefit is £5,500. He pays for all his own petrol.

(3) On 7 April 2013 he received a bonus of £5,000 which related to the sales he had made in the year ended 31 December 2012.

(4) He received a dividend from Jay plc of £9,900 in June 2013. This is the cash amount received.

(5) During 2013/14 Arkan received £600 interest from a building society and £400 interest from a cash ISA

(6) He pays 5% of his salary into a personal pension scheme.

Complete the following table to calculate Arkan's taxable income for 2013/14. You should use whole pounds only. If your answer is zero please include '0'. Do not use brackets or minus signs.

	£
Salary	
Personal pension scheme	
Bonus	
Car benefit	
Dividend	
Building society interest	
Interest from ISA	
Personal allowance	
Taxable income	

53 PHLOX

Phlox who is aged 86 gives you the following information about his income tax for 2013/14.

(1) His annual pension was £15,000 until 31 December 2013 when it was increased by 2%.

(2) He received a dividend from Enterprise plc of £4,500 in June 2013 and a dividend of £900 from shares held in an ISA. These are the cash amounts received.

(3) During 2013/14 Phlox received £6,000 interest from a building society and £805 interest from an NS&I bank account

(4) Phlox makes a payment of £400 to Oxfam each year under the Gift Aid scheme.

(5) Phlox sold shares during the year making a gain of £4,150

Complete the following table to calculate Phlox's taxable income for 2013/14. You should use whole pounds only. If your answer is zero please include '0'. Do not use brackets or minus signs.

	£
Pension	
Dividend from Enterprise plc	
ISA dividend	
Building society interest	
NS& I bank interest	
Gift Aid payment	
Gain on shares	
Personal allowance	
Taxable income	

54 ALEXIS

Alexis who is aged 35 gives you the following information about her income tax for 2013/14.

(1) Her annual salary was £40,000 until 1 September 2013 when she received a pay rise of £2,000 per annum.

(2) Alexis receives a commission based on 1% of sales she has made for the year ended 31 December. This is paid annually to her on the following 1 May. The sales she has made are as follows:

Year ended 31 December 2012	£120,000
Year ended 31 December 2013	£135,000

(3) Alexis does not have the use of a company car but is paid a mileage allowance of 35 pence per mile for every business mile. She travelled 14,000 business miles during 2013/14

(4) She received a dividend from Ark plc of £900 in August 2013. This is the cash amount received.

(5) During 2013/14 Alexis received £350 interest from a building society and £400 interest from a cash ISA

(6) She pays 5% of her salary into her employer's pension scheme. Her employers pay an amount equal to 6% of her salary into the scheme.

Complete the following table to calculate Arkan's taxable income for 2013/14. You should use whole pounds only. If your answer is zero please include '0'. Do not use brackets or minus signs.

	£
Salary	
Commission	
Contribution to employer pension scheme	
Employer's pension contribution	
Mileage allowance – taxable amount	
Mileage allowance – tax allowable expense	
Dividend	
Building society interest	
Interest from ISA	
Personal allowance	
Taxable income	

55 DOMINIC

Dominic has a salary of £45,000 with no other income or tax allowable expenses. He wants to start paying 7% of his salary into a personal pension scheme during 2013/14.

Explain to Dominic how he will get tax relief on his contribution, what effect this will have on his tax liability for 2013/14 and the net after tax cost of making his contribution (i.e. cash paid less any tax saved).

COMPUTATION OF TAX PAYABLE AND PAYMENT OF TAX

Key answer tips

Task 6 in the AQ2013 assessment will cover this area and be worth a maximum of 10 marks.

56 ROGER

Roger was born on 1 June 1935. During 2013/14 he receives a pension of £24,050, property income of £3,000 and dividends of £1,030.

Use the table below to calculate Roger's income tax liability for 2013/14.

57 RAY

Ray was born on 1 July 1942. During 2013/14 he receives income of £26,900 (gross amount) and cash dividends of £900. He made a Gift Aid payment of £400 in May 2013.

Use the table below to calculate Ray's income tax liability for 2013/14.

58 JJ

JJ was born on 1 September 1974. During 2013/14 he had employment income of £148,200, received building society interest of £5,720 and dividends of £6,800.

Use the table below to calculate JJ's income tax liability for 2013/14.

59 BILL

During 2013/14 Bill (born on 1 August 1980) had employment income of £10,500 (PAYE deducted of £150) and received building society interest of £2,400.

Use the table below to calculate Bill's income tax payable/repayable for 2013/14.

60 FENFANG

Fenfang was born on 1 December 1980. During 2013/14 she received £70,000 salary (gross amount) and £36,180 of dividends (none from ISAs).

She paid a personal pension scheme contribution of £2,000 and Gift Aid payments to charity totalling £160. PAYE of £25,100 was deducted from her salary.

Use the table below to calculate Fenfang's income tax payable for 2013/14.

THEORY UNDERPINNING TOPIC AND PENALTIES

Key answer tips

Task 7 in the AQ2013 assessment will cover this area and be worth a maximum of 10 marks. All or part of the question will require a free text written response. The task may have two or three parts. The questions in this section of the kit give practice on the individual parts likely to be tested in this task.

61 SADIE

One of your clients, Sadie, has written you an email dated 20 November 2014.

> "Hi, I know that I am a new client to your practice and that you did not prepare my tax return for 2012/13, but I have just realised that I failed to let HMRC know about some property income that I received in the first few months of 2013.
>
> I had assumed that since I had a lot of expenses in relation to the buy-to-let property, that they would outweigh the income and thus there was no need to inform them. I am now worried that HMRC will find out that I have not paid the right amount of tax on this income.
>
> Can you please advise about what I should do and about any penalties that I may incur?
>
> Regards, Sadie."

You need to respond appropriately to her query.

62 CHARLOTTE

Charlotte is a new client and has written to you with the following query dated 1 November 2014.

'I wonder if you could explain a few things for me about tax payments. My previous accountants gave me the following information for 2013/14:

	£
Income tax liability	14,580
Less: Tax deducted at source	(5,250)
	9,330
Capital gains tax liability	4,900
Tax payable	14,230

I never used to pay any tax by instalments but I paid £4,000 tax on 31 January 2014 and again on 31 July 2014. I don't understand how much I will have to pay on 31 January 2015.

Please can you tell me how much I will have to pay by that date and what happens if I pay my tax late.'

You need to respond appropriately to her query.

63 KATIE

Katie has written to you with the following query:

> 'I am writing to you as I have started to receive rental income from June 2013.
>
> I have been sent a tax return to complete for 2013/14. I have never filled in a return before as all my tax has been dealt with by my employer.
>
> Can you please reply answering the following queries?
>
> - When does my 2013/14 return need to be submitted and what are the penalties if I do not meet this deadline?
> - When are my payments of income tax due and what are the consequences if I pay late?
>
> Many thanks, Katie.'

You need to respond appropriately to her query.

64 CHARLIE

Charlie has written to you with the following query:

> 'I am writing to you for some clarification on my tax liabilities. Although I have been paying tax for a long time I still do not understand what needs paying and when.
>
> My tax liability was £8,600 for 2012/13. According to your calculation I will owe £9,000 for 2013/14.
>
> Could you please explain to me how my payments are calculated, and what they should have been for 2013/14 so I can check the HMRC figures.
>
> Many thanks for your time.
>
> Charlie

You need to respond appropriately to his query.

65 SOPHIA

You have received the following e-mail from Sophia dated 14 September 2014.

> I am a bit worried as I have been receiving interest from a loan to my brother but have never told you about it because I thought it was a private arrangement and not taxable. However my brother says I should have included it on my tax return.
>
> He first started paying me interest in June 2012 so I suppose it should have been included on my 2012/13 tax return. As you are still working on my 2013/14 return it will not be a problem to alter that.
>
> Please advise what we should do now and the consequences of this mistake. The interest was £1,500 in 2012/13 and £1,800 in 2013/14.

You should reply to Sophia's email. Sophia is a higher rate taxpayer.

66 JOHNSON

Johnson asks you which of the following statements are true.

(i) All tax returns must be filed by 31 October following the end of the tax year.

(ii) Taxpayers have the right to amend a return up to 18 months from 31 January following the end of the tax year.

A (i) only

B (ii) only

C Both of them

D Neither of them

67 ETHICAL RULES (1)

(a) Which ONE of the following statements is not correct?

A Accountants must not associate themselves with returns which contain false or misleading statements

B Accountants should not be associated with returns which contain information provided recklessly without any real knowledge of whether they are true or false

C Accountants are allowed to be associated with returns which may omit information which would mislead HMRC

D Accountants are obliged to not be associated with returns which may obscure information which would mislead HMRC

(b) When an accountant is giving a client advice, with whom can he share the information? Choose one option.

A HMRC

B Other clients with identical circumstances

C The client

68 ETHICAL RULES (2)

(a) Which ONE of the following statements is not correct?

A Accountants should not be involved with tax returns that omit information

B Accountants should not be associated with a return that contains misleading information

C Accountants who are involved with returns that deliberately contain false information can be subject to a penalty

D Accountants should never prepare tax returns for clients

(b) When can an accountant divulge confidential information?

A If the information is over 6 years old

B If a member of the public asks for it

C If the accountant has written authority from the client to disclose

D If the client's spouse requests the information

69 LAREDO

Laredo asks whether the following statements are true or false.

Tick the appropriate box for each statement.

	True	False
HMRC does not send out a tax return to all individuals.		
All tax records for an individual should be kept for at least 4 years.		
The maximum penalty for not keeping records is £2,000.		

70 CLIENT ADVICE

(a) Which ONE of the following statements is not correct?

A Accountants need to follow the rules of confidentiality unless given permission by a client

B Accountants can break the rules of confidentiality when the public interest is threatened

C Tax evasion is a legal means of reducing your tax liability

D The AAT expects its members to maintain an objective outlook

(b) When an accountant is advising a client, to whom does he owe the greatest duty of care?

A The accountant's employer

B The AAT

C The client

D The government

71 NEW SOURCES OF INCOME

Mark the following statements as either true or false.

	True	False
An individual who does not normally receive a tax return is responsible for letting HMRC know if they have a new source of income.		
Tax on chargeable gains is paid in two instalments on 31 January in the tax year and 31 July following the end of the tax year.		

72 AAT STUDENT

(a) Which of the following statements is not correct?

A As a student of the AAT you are bound by the duty of confidentiality

B The rules of confidentiality do not need to be followed when a wife asks for information about her husband's tax matters

C The rules of confidentiality need to be followed even after the client relationship has ended

D Confidentiality means not disclosing information you acquire due to your job

(b) When an accountant is working for a client, when can the rules of confidentiality be breached?

A If you do not agree with what the client is saying

B If the client refuses to correct an error in their tax return

C If you resign

D If the client is suspected of money laundering

73 FILING DEADLINES

Mark the following statements as either true or false.

	True	False
The filing deadline for 2013/14 paper returns is 31 October 2014.		
If you want to submit your 2013/14 tax return online, you must submit it by 31 January 2014.		

74 NASHEEN

Nasheen is a student member of the AAT. She asks whether the following statements are true or false.

Tick the appropriate box for each statement.

	True	False
If a husband is ill, it is acceptable to discuss their tax affairs with their wife even if no letter of authorisation exists.		
Accountants must follow the rules of confidentiality irrespective of the situation.		

75 ZAHERA

Mark the following statements as either true or false.

	True	False
Barclay filed his 2012/13 tax return electronically on 20 March 2014. The return showed tax outstanding of £186. Barclay will be charged a late filing penalty of £100.		
Caroli was due to pay a balancing payment of £4,200 on 31 January 2014. This was actually paid on 21 March 2014. Caroli will be charged interest from 31 January to 20 March.		
If a return is filed late then a late filing penalty is always charged, even if a taxpayer has a reasonable excuse.		

76 EMPLOYMENT STATUS

For each statement, tick either employment or self employment.

	Employment	Self employment
Contract for services is for		
Contract of service is for		
A worker providing their own tools to perform the work would indicate		

77 EMPLOYMENT OR SELF EMPLOYMENT (1)

For each statement, tick either employment or self employment.

	Employment	Self employment
Minimal degree of control exercised		
Being personally responsible for poor work		
Provision of sick and holiday pay		
Being able to hire helpers		
Carrying out an engagement for a long period		
Regular payment on a monthly basis		

78 EMPLOYMENT OR SELF EMPLOYMENT (2)

For each statement, tick either employment or self employment.

	Employment	Self employment
Being able to refuse work		
Being committed to work a specified number of hours at fixed times		
Being able to profit from sound management		
Having to carry out work yourself without being able to arrange for someone else to do it		
Having to provide your own equipment		
Not taking any financial risk		

79 TAX RETURN RESPONSIBILITY

Who is ultimately responsible for ensuring that a taxpayer's tax return is accurately completed?

A HMRC

B Tax adviser

C Taxpayer

D HM Treasury

80 MAXIMUM PENALTIES

Complete the boxes below with the maximum penalty that may be levied:

Failure to keep records to support the tax return	
Being one month late in filing an income tax return	
Being 2 months late in paying a balancing payment of £4,000	

81 REASONABLE EXCUSE

Which of the following is considered a reasonable excuse to reduce or cancel a penalty for filing an electronic tax return late?

Select one answer

A You did not realise that the deadline was 31 January

B Your accountant failed to deal with your return in time

C Your computer system broke down during December

D You were seriously ill throughout January

82 PENALTY TABLE

Fill in the gaps in the following table of penalties for incorrect returns:

	Maximum penalty	**Minimum penalties**	
		Unprompted disclosure	**Prompted disclosure**
	% of tax lost	**% of tax lost**	**% of tax lost**
Failure to take reasonable care	30%		15%
Deliberate understatement		20%	
Deliberate understatement with concealment	100%		50%

TAX RETURNS

Key answer tips

Task 8 in the AQ2013 assessment will cover this area and be worth a maximum of 7 marks.

83 MELANIE

Complete the tax return below as far as is possible using the following information.

Melanie had a salary of £30,000 for 2013/14 with PAYE deducted of £5,146. She also had the following assessable benefits and allowable expenses from her employment during 2013/14:

Private health cover	£385
Mileage rate scheme shortfall	£200
Company van	£3,000
Interest free loan	£900
Professional subscription	£250

Employment

Tax year 6 April 2013 to 5 April 2014

Your name

Your Unique Taxpayer Reference (UTR)

Complete an *Employment* page for each employment or directorship

1 Pay from this employment – the total from your P45 or P60 – *before tax was taken off*

£ .00

2 UK tax taken off pay in box 1

£ .00

3 Tips and other payments not on your P60 – *read the Employment notes*

£ .00

4 PAYE tax reference of your employer (on your P45/P60)

/

5 Your employer's name

6 If you were a company director, put 'X' in the box

7 And, if the company was a close company, put 'X' in the box

8 If you are a part-time teacher in England or Wales and are on the Repayment of Teachers' Loans Scheme for this employment, put 'X' in the box

Benefits from your employment – use your form P11D (or equivalent information)

9 Company cars and vans – *the total 'cash equivalent' amount*

£ .00

10 Fuel for company cars and vans – *the total 'cash equivalent' amount*

£ .00

11 Private medical and dental insurance – *the total 'cash equivalent' amount*

£ .00

12 Vouchers, credit cards and excess mileage allowance

£ .00

13 Goods and other assets provided by your employer – *the total value or amount*

£ .00

14 Accommodation provided by your employer – *the total value or amount*

£ .00

15 Other benefits (including interest-free and low interest loans) – *the total 'cash equivalent' amount*

£ .00

16 Expenses payments received and balancing charges

£ .00

Employment expenses

17 Business travel and subsistence expenses

£ .00

18 Fixed deductions for expenses

£ .00

19 Professional fees and subscriptions

£ .00

20 Other expenses and capital allowances

£ .00

Shares schemes, employment lump sums, compensation, deductions and Seafarers' Earnings Deduction are on the *Additional information* pages enclosed in the tax return pack.

SA102 2013 Page E 1 HMRC 12/12

84 MICHAEL

Complete the tax return below as far as is possible using the following information.

Michael sold 3 lots of listed shares during 2013/14. These were his only capital disposals during 2013/14.

He has £4,700 of capital losses brought forward.

The summary information from these disposals is:

Shares	*Sale proceeds*	*Cost*
	£	£
May disposal	25,500	14,000
November disposal	10,000	7,000
January disposal	7,000	9,000

Capital gains summary

Tax year 6 April 2013 to 5 April 2014

1 Your name

2 Your Unique Taxpayer Reference (UTR)

Summary of your enclosed computations

Please read the *Capital gains summary notes* on pages CGN 10 to CGN 13 before filling in this section. **You must enclose your computations, including details of each gain or loss, as well as filling in the boxes.**

3 Total gains *(Boxes 19 + 25 + 31 + 32)*

£ ·00

4 Gains qualifying for Entrepreneurs' Relief (but excluding gains deferred from before 23 June 2010) *- read the notes on page CGN 11*

£ ·00

5 Gains invested under Seed Enterprise Investment Scheme and qualifying for exemption *- read the notes on page CGN 11 and 12*

£ ·00

6 **Total losses of the year** *- enter '0' if there are none*

£ ·00

7 Losses brought forward and used in the year

£ ·00

8 Adjustment to Capital Gains Tax *- read the notes*

£ ·00

9 Additional liability for non-resident or dual resident trusts

£ ·00

10 Losses available to be carried forward to later years

£ ·00

11 **Losses used against an earlier year's gain (special circumstances apply** *- read the notes on page CGN 12)*

£ ·00

12 Losses used against income – **amount claimed against 2013–14 income** *- read the notes on page CGN 13*

£ ·00

13 Losses used against income – **amount claimed against 2012–13 income** *- read the notes on page CGN 13*

£ ·00

14 Income losses of 2013–14 set against gains

£ ·00

15 Deferred gains from before 23 June 2010 qualifying for Entrepreneurs' Relief

£ ·00

Listed shares and securities

16 Number of disposals *- read the notes on page CGN 13*

17 Disposal proceeds

£ ·00

18 Allowable costs (including purchase price)

£ ·00

19 Gains in the year, before losses

£ ·00

20 If you are making any claim or election, put 'X' in the box

21 If your computations include any estimates or valuations, put 'X' in the box

SA108 2013 Page CG 1 HMRC 12/12

85 SULLIVAN

Complete the tax return below as far as the following information permits.

Sullivan works for Kharral Ltd. In 2013/14 he had a salary of £20,000 and paid PAYE of £4,200. He also had the following benefits:

Private medical insurance benefit	£600
Car benefit	£4,000
Fuel benefit	£3,500
Beneficial loan benefit	£300

Kharral Ltd provided Sullivan with a camera throughout 2013/14. The camera cost Kharral Ltd £2,250 and it is used by Sullivan for private purposes only.

Employment

Tax year 6 April 2013 to 5 April 2014

Your name

Your Unique Taxpayer Reference (UTR)

Complete an *Employment* page for each employment or directorship

1 Pay from this employment – the total from your P45 or P60 – *before tax was taken off*

£ • 0 0

2 UK tax taken off pay in box 1

£ • 0 0

3 Tips and other payments not on your P60 – *read the Employment notes*

£ • 0 0

4 PAYE tax reference of your employer (on your P45/P60)

/

5 Your employer's name

6 If you were a company director, put 'X' in the box

7 And, if the company was a close company, put 'X' in the box

8 If you are a part-time teacher in England or Wales and are on the Repayment of Teachers' Loans Scheme for this employment, put 'X' in the box

Benefits from your employment – use your form P11D (or equivalent information)

9 Company cars and vans – *the total 'cash equivalent' amount*

£ • 0 0

10 Fuel for company cars and vans – *the total 'cash equivalent' amount*

£ • 0 0

11 Private medical and dental insurance – *the total 'cash equivalent' amount*

£ • 0 0

12 Vouchers, credit cards and excess mileage allowance

£ • 0 0

13 Goods and other assets provided by your employer – *the total value or amount*

£ • 0 0

14 Accommodation provided by your employer – *the total value or amount*

£ • 0 0

15 Other benefits (including interest-free and low interest loans) – *the total 'cash equivalent' amount*

£ • 0 0

16 Expenses payments received and balancing charges

£ • 0 0

Employment expenses

17 Business travel and subsistence expenses

£ • 0 0

18 Fixed deductions for expenses

£ • 0 0

19 Professional fees and subscriptions

£ • 0 0

20 Other expenses and capital allowances

£ • 0 0

Shares schemes, employment lump sums, compensation, deductions and Seafarers' Earnings Deduction are on the *Additional information* pages enclosed in the tax return pack.

SA102 2013 Page E 1 HMRC 12/12

86 GUILLE

Guille gives you the following information about his furnished property for 2013/14. This is not classed as furnished holiday accommodation.

	£
Rents	76,320
Expenses:	
Insurance	5,580
Water rates	336
Council tax	3,900
Cleaning	7,300
Redecoration	5,000

Complete the tax return below as far as the above information permits.

Property income

Do not include furnished holiday lettings, Real Estate Investment Trust or Property Authorised Investment Funds dividends/ distributions here.

20 **Total rents and other income from property**

£ .00

21 **Tax taken off any income in box 20**

£ .00

22 **Premiums for the grant of a lease – from box E on the Working Sheet** – *read the notes*

£ .00

23 **Reverse premiums and inducements**

£ .00

Property expenses

24 **Rent, rates, insurance, ground rents etc.**

£ .00

25 **Property repairs, maintenance and renewals**

£ .00

26 **Loan interest and other financial costs**

£ .00

27 **Legal, management and other professional fees**

£ .00

28 **Costs of services provided, including wages**

£ .00

29 **Other allowable property expenses**

£ .00

Calculating your taxable profit or loss

30 **Private use adjustment** – *read the notes*

£ .00

31 **Balancing charges** – *read the notes*

£ .00

32 **Annual Investment Allowance**

£ .00

33 **Business Premises Renovation Allowance (Assisted Areas only)** – *read the notes*

£ .00

34 **All other capital allowances**

£ .00

35 **Landlord's Energy Saving Allowance**

£ .00

36 **10% wear and tear allowance** – *for furnished residential accommodation only*

£ .00

37 **Rent a Room exempt amount**

£ .00

38 **Adjusted profit for the year – from box O on the Working Sheet** – *read the notes*

£ .00

39 **Loss brought forward used against this year's profits**

£ .00

40 **Taxable profit for the year (box 38 minus box 39)**

£ .00

41 **Adjusted loss for the year – from box O on the Working Sheet** – *read the notes*

£ .00

42 **Loss set off against 2013–14 total income** – *this will be unusual – read the notes*

£ .00

43 **Loss to carry forward to following year, including unused losses brought forward**

£ .00

SA105 2013 Page UKP 2

CHARGEABLE GAINS

BASICS OF CAPITAL GAINS TAX

Key answer tips

Task 9 in the AQ2013 assessment will cover this area and be worth a maximum of 10 marks. The task may have two or three parts. The questions in this section of the kit give practice on the individual parts likely to be tested in this task.

87 CONNECTED PERSONS

For each statement, tick the appropriate box.

	Actual proceeds used	Deemed proceeds used	No gain / no loss basis
(a) Sister gives an asset to her brother			
(b) Civil partner gives an asset to civil partner			
(c) Luke sells an asset to his friend for £38,000. He later discovers the asset is worth £45,000.			

88 HARRY AND BETSY

(a) Harry bought a second property as an investment in February 2009 for £155,000. He built a conservatory costing £15,000 and an extension which cost £28,000 during 2010.

In March 2014 he sold the entire property for £400,000.

What is the gain on this asset?

A £400,000

B £245,000

C £202,000

D £155,000

(b) Betsy bought an antique set of 6 chairs in August 2011 for £15,000, and then sold two of them in January 2014 for £10,000. The market value of the remaining 4 chairs is £25,000.

In the chargeable gain calculation what is the allowable cost of the two chairs sold?

A £6,250

B £5,714

C £5,000

D £4,286

(c) True or False:

Auctioneers fees are never an allowable deduction from sales proceeds.

89 SAMANTHA

For each statement, tick the appropriate box.

	Actual proceeds used	Deemed proceeds used	No gain no loss basis
(a) Samantha sells an asset to her colleague for £8,000. She then discovers that it was worth £10,000			
(b) Neil sells an asset to his wife for £10,000 when the market value is £14,000			
(c) Simon gives an asset to his friend.			

90 JAY AND CARLI

(a) Jay bought a building in September 2010 for £70,000. He spent £10,000 on repairs to the building in June 2011 and sold it for £120,000 in July 2013.

What is the gain on this asset?

(b) Carli bought an asset in May 2006 for £50,000, selling it in November 2013 for £30,000. She paid auctioneer's commission of 4% when she bought the asset and 5% when she sold the asset.

What is the loss on this asset?

(c) True or false:

If shares are bought for £3,000 and sold for proceeds of £5,000 then the gain of £2,000 is not chargeable.

91 VICTORIA

Victoria holds a party which is attended by many people including;

Cecil – her husband

Mike – married to Victoria's daughter

Janet – her sister

Alice – Janet's daughter

Tim – her bank manager

Olive – her cousin

How many of these people are connected with Victoria for capital gains purposes?

A 2

B 3

C 4

D 5

92 JACOB

Jacob bought an asset in October 2007 for £180,000. He spent £10,000 on repairs in June 2009 and £60,000 on improvements in May 2011. He sold the asset for £300,000 in September 2013.

What is the gain on this asset?

A £60,000

B £120,000

C £50,000

D £230,000

93 ESHE

Eshe made the following capital disposals in 2013/14.

(i) Sold a necklace worth £50,000 to her sister for £40,000. The necklace had cost Eshe £31,500 in June 2003.

(ii) Gave shares in X plc, a quoted trading company, to her husband's brother. The shares cost £16,700 and were worth £9,000 at the time of the gift.

(iii) Sold an antique table costing £8,000 to her cousin for £11,000. £11,000 was the price that an antique dealer had offered to Eshe earlier in the year. Later Eshe discovered its value was in fact £12,000.

No other capital disposals were made.

What is the total of Eshe's taxable gains for 2013/14?

A £2,900

B £3,900

C £11,600

D £10,600

94 KAMILAH

(a) Kamilah owned an antique clock which she bought for £25,000 in May 2003. In September 2013 the clock was destroyed in a fire and she received £48,000 in insurance proceeds.

What is the gain/loss (if any) on this asset? ....

(b) Kamilah owned a set of three paintings. She had bought these in October 2005 for £16,500 in total. She sold one of the paintings in November 2013 for £20,000. The remaining two paintings had a total market value of £36,000.

What is the gain/loss (if any) on this asset? ....

95 ALVIN

Alvin bought a 10 acre field in May 2004 for £40,000. In June 2013 he sold 4 acres for £83,000 net of £2,000 selling expenses. The remaining 6 acres were valued at £110,000.

In December 2013 Alvin sold the remaining 6 acres of land for £118,000 which was the gross proceeds before incurring £1,500 selling expenses.

(a)	What is the gain/loss on the disposal in June 2013?	
(b)	What is the gain/loss on the disposal in December 2013?	

96 BEN

Ben has disposed of the non-wasting chattels below.

Calculate the gain/loss on each.

Asset	Sale proceeds	Cost	Gain/Loss
1	£5,000	£4,000	
2	£10,000	£7,000	
3	£9,000	£3,000	
4	£4,000	£9,000	

97 CHATTELS – MARGINAL GAIN

On which of the following disposals is the gain calculated using the chattel marginal gain rules?

Tick the appropriate box for each disposal.

	Applies	Does not apply
A racehorse bought for £4,000 and sold for £7,500		
A necklace bought for £5,900 plus £200 of auction costs, and given away when its market value was £8,000		
An antique vase bought for £3,000 and sold for £8,200		
A painting bought for £3,000 and sold for £5,900		
Shares bought for £2,100 and sold for £6,900		

98 MATCHING STATEMENTS

Match the following statements to the appropriate asset details.

All assets are non-wasting chattels.

Note you may use a statement more than once.

Asset	Sale proceeds	Cost	Statement
1	£12,000	£18,000	
2	£5,000	£6,000	
3	£8,000	£4,000	
4	£7,000	£6,500	
5	£5,000	£7,000	

Statements:

(i) Exempt asset disposal

(ii) Calculate gain as normal

(iii) Calculate loss as normal

(iv) Sale proceeds deemed to be £6,000

(v) Marginal gain restriction applies

99 MARTOK

Martok has disposed of the following assets.

Which are exempt?

	Exempt	Not exempt
A bravery medal he inherited from his father.		
A quarter share in a racehorse		
Antique violin sold for £150,000		
His personal computer		
Shares held in an ISA		

TAXATION OF SHARES

Key answer tips

Task 10 in the AQ2013 assessment will cover this area and be worth a maximum of 8 marks.

100 STRINGER LTD

John bought 8,000 shares in Stringer Ltd for £8 per share in July 2006. In March 2007 he purchased a further 4,000 shares for £9 each and in July 2009 he sold 3,000 shares for £20,000. In May 2013 he received a 1 for 1 bonus issue.

In February 2014 John sold 5,000 shares for £10 per share.

Clearly showing the balance of shares, and their value, to carry forward calculate the gain made on the shares sold in February 2014.

All workings must be shown in your calculations.

101 LULU LTD

Peter bought 12,000 shares in Lulu Ltd for £4 per share in October 2004. He received a bonus issue of 1 for 12 shares in June 2006 and in April 2010 he sold 3,000 shares for £5 per share.

In January 2014, Peter sold 8,000 shares for £7 per share.

Clearly showing the balance of shares, and their value, to carry forward calculate the gain made on the shares sold in January 2014.

All workings must be shown in your calculations.

102 GILBERT LTD

Phil bought 8,000 shares in Gilbert Ltd for £4 per share in May 2003. He received a bonus issue of 1 for 4 shares in June 2007. In July 2009 he bought an additional 2,000 shares for £8 a share. On 7 September 2013, Phil sold 8,000 shares for £65,000 and on 15 September 2013 he bought 2,200 shares for £20,000.

Clearly showing the balance of shares, and their value, to carry forward calculate the gain made on these shares.

All workings must be shown in your calculations.

103 BELLA

Bella bought 16,000 shares in Nessie Ltd for £6 per share on 9 September 2006. She took advantage of a rights issue of 1 for 8 shares at £4 a share on 14 June 2010. On 14 May 2013, Bella sold 9,000 shares for £11 per share. On 17 May 2013 Bella bought 1,000 shares for £10 per share.

Clearly showing the balance of shares, and their value, to carry forward calculate the gain made on these shares.

All workings must be shown in your calculations.

104 BAJOR PLC

Mohamed has the following transactions in the shares of Bajor plc:

		Number of shares	*Cost/proceeds*
February 2004	Purchased	2,000	£7,560
July 2006	Bonus issue	1 for 10	
December 2008	Purchased	500	£2,800
April 2010	Rights issue	1 for 5	£2.50 per share
March 2014	Sold	2,500	£17,500

Clearly showing the balance of shares, and their value, to carry forward calculate the gain or loss made on these shares.

All workings must be shown in your calculations.

CAPITAL GAINS TAX EXEMPTIONS, LOSSES, RELIEFS AND TAX PAYABLE

Key answer tips

Task 11 in the AQ2013 assessment will cover this area and be worth a maximum of 6 marks. The task may have two or three parts. The questions in this section of the kit give practice on the individual parts likely to be tested in this task.

105 GARIBALDI

Advise Garibaldi whether the following statements are true or false.

Tick the appropriate box for each statement.

	True	False
Brought forward capital losses cannot be used before current year capital losses.		
Excess capital losses can be used against other income.		
Capital gains are taxed at 40% for higher rate taxpayers.		

106 JR

JR, born on 1 April 1990, has an annual salary of £40,000 for 2013/14 and no other income.

He sold a painting in December 2013 for £25,620 which he originally purchased for £8,500 in August 2007. He paid 2% commission on the sale. This was his only capital disposal in 2013/14.

What is JR's capital gains tax payable for 2013/14?

A £1,453.24

B £1,027.44

C £1,598.24

D £4,505.24

107 ANGELA

Angela bought an asset in May 2009 for £150,000. She spent £30,000 on enhancing this asset in April 2011 and sold the asset for £290,000 in March 2014.

Angela made no other capital disposals in 2013/14.

She has taxable income of £20,810 and made a Gift Aid payment of £400 in 2013/14.

What is her capital gains tax liability for 2013/14?

A £26,628.00

B £26,578.00

C £27,748.00

D £29,680.00

108 KIESWETTER

(a) True or false:

All animals are exempt from capital gains tax.

(b) True or false:

Vintage cars are chargeable assets for CGT purposes.

(c) Kieswetter has capital gains for 2013/14 of £20,000 and capital losses of £5,200. He also has capital losses brought forward of £7,000.

What capital loss (if any) can he carry forward to 2014/15?

A £Nil

B £3,100

C £3,900

D £7,000

109 JOANNA

Advise Joanna whether the following statements are true or false.

Tick the appropriate box for each statement.

	True	False
Capital gains are taxed at 18% for all taxpayers.		
If a taxpayer does not use their annual exempt amount in 2012/13 they can bring it forward to use in 2013/14.		
Brought forward capital losses are restricted to allow full use of the annual exempt amount for the year.		

110 ALICE

Alice bought an asset in May 2006 for £35,700, selling it in December 2013 for £52,000.

She paid auctioneers commission of 2% when she sold the asset and legal fees of £250 when she bought it.

Alice has made no other capital disposals in 2013/14 and is a higher rate taxpayer.

She paid her accountant £100 to calculate her capital gains tax liability on this disposal.

What is her capital gains tax liability for 2013/14?

111 KEVIN

Kevin has made the following statements. Which of them are true?

(i) Unused personal allowance can be deducted from taxable gains.

(ii) Current year capital losses can be restricted to protect the annual exempt amount.

(iii) A capital loss made on a disposal to a connected person can only be deducted from gains on disposals to the same connected person.

A (i) only

B (ii) only

C (iii) only

D (i) and (iii)

112 RASHIDA

In each of the following cases, calculate how much capital loss is available to carry forward to 2014/15

	Capital loss b/f £	*Capital gain 2013/14* £	*Capital loss 2013/14* £	*Capital loss c/f* £
1	7,560	25,000	12,290	
2	Nil	16,500	21,000	
3	12,900	14,780	8,000	
4	5,200	13,700	Nil	

113 ARLENE

Arlene has £31,500 of gains and £4,500 of capital losses for 2013/14. She has £7,200 of her basic rate band unused.

What is her capital gains tax liability for 2013/14?

When will this tax be payable?

114 HUEY, DUEY AND LOUIE

The capital gains for three taxpayers for 2013/14 are shown in the table below, together with their capital losses brought forward from 2012/13. The gains are before deduction of the annual exempt amount.

Tick the relevant box to show how the losses brought forward will be relieved in 2013/14.

Taxpayer	**Gain 2013/14**	**Loss 2012/13 b/f**	**Relieve all loss**	**Relieve some loss**	**Relieve no loss**
Huey	£21,450	£6,550			
Duey	£10,230	£5,150			
Louie	£14,790	£7,820			

115 TINEKE

Tineke bought a flat on 31 May 2005 for £99,000.

She lived in the house until 31 December 2005 when she moved abroad to work for two years.

Her employer then moved her to another region of England for a secondment when she returned, and this lasted 8 months.

She then moved back into the flat on 1 September 2008 but this was short-lived and she moved out again to live with her boyfriend on 1 December 2008.

She sold the flat on 31 December 2013.

Which periods are treated as occupied and which are not?

Occupation	Non-occupation

116 RENATA

Renata bought a house on 1 May 2003 for £50,000.

She lived in the house until 31 December 2006 when she moved in with her sister.

The house remained unoccupied until she sold it on 1 July 2013 for £180,000.

This house is Renata's only property.

Which periods are treated as occupied and which are not?

Occupation	Non-occupation

117 YASMIN

Which of the following absences would be treated as occupation or part occupation of a principal private residence?

Assume that in each case the owner spent all other periods occupying the property, both before and after the absence, unless told otherwise.

	All treated as occupation	Part treated as occupation	Not treated as occupation
(a) Yasmin spent 10 years working abroad.			
(b) George spent 4 years motorcycling around the world.			
(c) The last 4 years of Owen's ownership in which he did not live in the house.			
(d) Ian spent 5 years working elsewhere in the UK			
(e) Irina moved out of her house and spent 2 years living in her boyfriend's house. After they split up she moved back to live with her parents and never moved back to her own house which she sold 5 years later. – for the 2 years living with boyfriend – for the 5 years living with parents			

118 ESME

Esme bought a house on 1 July 2003 for £40,000.

She lived in the house until 30 June 2005 when she left to travel the world for a year.

She then moved back in until 30 June 2008 when she left to move in with her boyfriend.

The house remained unoccupied until she sold it on 1 July 2013 for £285,000.

This house is Esme's only property.

Which periods are treated as occupied and which are not?

(a)	The total period of ownership of the house is (in months)	
(b)	The period of actual and deemed residence is (in months)	
(c)	The chargeable gain on the sale of the house is (to the nearest £)	

119 LYNNETTE

Lynnette sold her private residence making a gain of £360,000.

She had owned the house for 20 years.

The first 8 years she lived in the house and then as her employer relocated his business, she went to work in Scotland. She lived in rented accommodation in Scotland and never returned to her own house.

What is the capital gain on the sale of Lynnette's private residence?

£.......................................

Section 2

ANSWERS TO PRACTICE QUESTIONS

INCOME TAX

ASSESSABLE BENEFITS – PROVISION OF CARS

1 SNAPE

(a) Car benefit percentages

(i) The answer is 10%.

Tutorial note

The car has CO_2 emissions of between 76 and 94 g/km and is therefore a low emission car.

The appropriate percentage is 10% for a petrol car and 13% for a diesel car.

(ii) The answer is 16%.

CO_2 emissions are rounded down to 120 g/km.

Appropriate percentage = (11% petrol + (120 – 95) × 1/5) = 16%

(iii) The answer is 22%.

CO_2 emissions are rounded down to 150 g/km.

Appropriate percentage = (11% petrol + (150 – 95) × 1/5) = 22%

(iv) The answer is 35%.

CO_2 emissions are rounded down to 235 g/km.

Appropriate percentage = (11% petrol + (235 – 95) × 1/5) = 39%

However, the maximum percentage is 35%.

Tutorial note

The cars in (ii) to (iv) have CO_2 emissions in excess of 95 g/km.

The appropriate percentage is therefore calculated in the normal way (i.e. a scale percentage of 11% for petrol cars and 14% for diesel cars, plus 1% for each 5 completed emissions above 95 g/km up to a maximum percentage of 35%).

(b) Snape's car

(i) The scale percentage for the car is 25%.

Scale for a 154 g/km petrol car is 22% (see a (iii) above).

A diesel car has an extra 3% added.

(ii) The cost of the car to use in the assessable benefit calculation is the list price of £21,995.

(iii) The standard amount on which the fuel benefit is calculated in 2012/13

= £21,100.

(iv) Fuel benefit = (£21,100 × 25%) = £5,275

Key answer tips

Note that a mark would be given in part (iv) if you calculated the benefit based on your answers to (i) and (iii).

Tutorial note

Car benefits are calculated as follows:

- *Scale percentage × List price × n/12*
- *Where n = number of months the car is available in the tax year.*

The scale percentage is found from the following calculation:

- *11% + (CO_2 emissions – 95) × 1/5*
- *CO_2 emissions are rounded down to the next number ending in 0 or 5.*
- *Diesel cars attract an extra 3%*
- *Maximum scale percentage is 35%.*

Fuel benefit is calculated as follows:

- *Scale percentage × £21,100 × n/12*
- *Where n = number of months the benefit is available in the tax year.*

If an employee contributes towards the running costs of the car this is an allowable deduction, but partial contributions towards the cost of private fuel are NOT an allowable deduction.

2 SAM

(a) Scale charges

(i) The answer = 10%

Tutorial note

The car has CO_2 emissions of between 76 to 94 g/km and is therefore a low emission car.

The appropriate percentage for a petrol car is 10%, and 13% for a diesel car.

(ii) The answer = 8%

Tutorial note

The car has CO_2 emissions of less than 76 g/km and is therefore a very low emission car.

The appropriate percentage for a petrol car is 5%, and 8% for a diesel car.

(iii) The answer = 29%

CO_2 emissions are rounded down to 170 g/km.

Appropriate percentage = (14% diesel + (170 – 95) × 1/5) = 29%

Tutorial note

The car has CO_2 emissions in excess of 95 g/km.

The appropriate percentage is therefore calculated in the normal way (i.e. a scale percentage of 11% for petrol cars and 14% for diesel cars, plus 1% for each 5 completed emissions above 95 g/km up to a maximum percentage of 35%).

(iv) The answer = 35%

CO_2 emissions are rounded down to 220 g/km.

Appropriate percentage = (11% petrol + (220 – 95) × 1/5) = 36%

However, the maximum percentage is 35%.

Tutorial note

The car has CO_2 emissions in excess of 95 g/km.

The appropriate percentage is therefore calculated in the normal way (i.e. a scale percentage of 11% for petrol cars and 14% for diesel cars, plus 1% for each 5 completed emissions above 95 g/km up to a maximum percentage of 35%).

(b) Sam's car

(i) What is the scale charge percentage for this car? (W1)	30%
(ii) What is the cost of the car to use in the assessable benefit calculation? (W2)	£27,000
(iii) What is the amount of car running costs taxed on Sam in 2013/14?	£ Nil

Workings

(1) The CO_2 emissions are rounded down to 175 g/km.

Appropriate percentage = 14% diesel + (175 – 95) × 1/5 = 30%

(2) The benefit is based on the original list price.

Tutorial note

The scale percentage for diesel cars is 3% higher than for the equivalent petrol engine car but with the same maximum of 35%.

The car benefit covers all the running costs of the car except for the provision of private fuel and the services of a chauffeur.

Costs such as repairs, insurance, servicing and road tax are not assessed on the employee.

However, if an employee paid some of these expenses privately they could deduct the amount spent from their assessable car benefit.

3 FRODO

(a) The answer is B.

Tutorial note

Car benefits are calculated based on list price.

(b) The answer is 22%.

CO_2 emissions are rounded down to 150 g/km.

Appropriate percentage = (11% petrol + (150 – 95) × 1/5) = 22%

Tutorial note

The car has CO_2 emissions in excess of 95 g/km.

The appropriate percentage is therefore calculated in the normal way (i.e. a scale percentage of 11% for petrol cars and 14% for diesel cars, plus 1% for each 5 completed emissions above 95 g/km up to a maximum percentage of 35%).

(c) The answer is £3,253

Car benefit:

£26,000 × 22% × 8/12 (available from 5 August) less £560 (contribution for private use).

(d) The answer is £3,095

Fuel benefit = (£21,100 × 22% × 8/12)

Tutorial note

The £70 per month paid in respect of the private use of the car can be deducted from Tony's car benefit. The total amount deductible is £70 per month for eight months.

The £30 per month partial contribution towards private fuel cannot be deducted from the fuel benefit.

4 BARRY

(a) Barry's car

(i)	What is the scale charge percentage for this car? (W1)	29%
(ii)	What is the cost of the car to use in the assessable benefit calculation? (W2)	£22,000
(iii)	What is Barry's assessable car benefit in 2012/13? (W3)	£5,780

Workings

(1) CO_2 emissions are rounded down to 170 g/km.

Appropriate percentage = (14% diesel + (170 – 95) × 1/5 = 29%

(2) Cost of car

= (Manufacturer's list price less capital contribution made by employee)

but note that the maximum capital contribution deduction is £5,000.

= (£27,000 – £5,000 max) = £22,000

(3) Car benefit – car available throughout the whole year 2013/14

= (£22,000 × 29%) less (£50 × 12) employee contribution

Tutorial note

The car benefit covers all the running costs of the car except for the provision of private fuel and the services of a chauffeur.

Costs such as repairs, insurance, servicing and road tax are not assessed on the employee.

However, if an employee paid some of these expenses privately they could deduct the amount spent from their assessable car benefit.

(b) The answer is B.

Working

Fuel benefit = (£21,100 × 24% × 7/12) = £2,954

Tutorial note

The scale percentage for diesel cars is 3% higher than for the equivalent petrol engine car but with the same maximum of 35%.

The fuel benefit applies because Crouch receives private fuel and does not reimburse his employer the whole cost. Partial contributions towards private fuel are ignored.

The fuel benefit is based on a fixed figure of £21,100 in 2013/14.

The benefit is time apportioned because Crouch only has the car and fuel for 7 months during the tax year from 1 September 2013.

5 JACKIE

(a) Car benefit

(i)	What is the scale charge percentage for this car? (W1)	21 %
(ii)	What is the cost of the car to use in the assessable benefit calculation? (W2)	£ 13,900
(iii)	Jackie is not taxed on his car benefit for the 5 weeks during 2013/14 when the car is unavailable.	False
(iv)	What is Jackie's assessable car benefit for 2013/14?	£2,676

Workings

(1) CO_2 emissions are rounded down to 130 g/km.

Appropriate percentage = (14% diesel + (130 – 95) × 1/5) = 21%

(2) Cost of car = (£12,400 + £1,500 accessories) = £13,900

(3) Car benefit = (£13,900 × 21% × 11/12)

Tutorial note

The cost of the car to use in the assessable benefit calculation is the manufacturer's list price plus the cost of accessories purchased with the car, and those added at a later date (unless the accessory cost less than £100).

For the car benefit to be reduced, it must be unavailable for at least 30 consecutive days. Temporary non-availability of less than 30 days is ignored.

Since the car was first provided on 1 May 2013, the benefit only applies for 11 months.

(b) Pool car

	True	False
A pool car can be used exclusively by one employee		✓
A pool car is normally garaged at the company premises	✓	
A pool car should only be used for business travel	✓	

Tutorial note

There is no benefit where there is provision of a company car (and associated services) which is a 'pool' car.

A pool car is one which is not exclusively used by any one employee, and which is not available for travel from home to work, being garaged at company premises, and is only used for business travel.

ASSESSABLE BENEFITS – ALL EXCLUDING CARS

6 BRIAN

(a) The answer is £125.

Working

Use of asset benefit = (£750 × 20% × 10/12) = £125

Tutorial note

The benefit for use of a company asset such as a computer is 20% of the market value of the asset when first made available to the employee.

Brian has only had use of the laptop for 10 months in the tax year 2013/14, therefore the benefit must be time apportioned.

(b) The answer is £50.

Gift of asset after previous use of asset benefit = Higher of

(i) (£250 – £200) = £50, or

(ii) (£500 – £350 – £200) = £Nil

Tutorial note

When an asset previously used by an employee is sold or given to them the assessable benefit is calculated as follows.

***Higher** of:*

(i) Market value of asset at date of transfer to employee less price paid by employee

(ii) Original market value when first supplied as a benefit less amounts taxed as a benefit to date less price paid by employee.

(c) Job related accommodation

	Job related	**Not job related**
Accommodation provided for a lighthouse keeper	✓	
Accommodation provided for executive directors		✓
Accommodation provided for non-executive directors		✓

Tutorial note

*Accommodation provided for a lighthouse keeper is job related as it is **necessary** for the keeper to live in the lighthouse **in order to perform his duties** of employment.*

Accommodation supplied for directors can only be job related if special security considerations apply.

(d) The answer is C.

Working

	£
Annual value	3,250
Additional charge for 'expensive' accommodation:	
(£228,000 – £75,000) × 4.00% (Note)	6,120
	9,370
Time apportion – from 1.8.2013 to 5.4.2014 (£9,370 × 8/12)	6,247
Less: Rent paid by Esme (£100 × 8 months)	(800)
Assessable benefit – 2013/14	5,447

Tutorial note

The house was purchased by Esme's employers in June 2006 and Esme moved in on 1 August 2013.

The house had therefore been owned by the employers for more than six years when Esme first moved in.

Accordingly, the expensive accommodation benefit must be calculated using the market value of the house when Esme first moved in rather than the original cost.

7 LOACH

(a) The answer is B.

Tutorial note

Interest free and low interest loans which do not exceed £5,000 at any time in the tax year are an exempt benefit.

(b) The answer is A.

Working

Expensive accommodation benefit

= ((£100,000 + £30,500) – £75,000) × 4.00% = £2,220

Tutorial note

The house was purchased by Margarita's employers in December 2007 and Margarita moved in on 1 November 2012.

The house had therefore been owned by the employers for less than six years when Margarita first moved in.

Accordingly, the expensive accommodation benefit must be calculated using the original cost of the house plus improvements up to the start of the tax year, and not the market value when Margarita first moved in.

The house has been available for the whole of the tax year 2013/14, therefore there is no need to time apportion the benefit.

(c) Job related accommodation

	Job related	Not job related
Accommodation provided for a member of the clergy	✓	
Accommodation provided for a zookeeper at Dudley Zoo	✓	
Accommodation provided for directors to enable them to get to work more easily		✓

Tutorial note

Accommodation provided for a zoo keeper and for a member of the clergy is job related as it is provided for the ***better performance of their duties*** *and it is* ***customary*** *for such employments to be provided with accommodation.*

Accommodation supplied for directors can only be job related if special security considerations apply.

(d) The answer is C.

Working

		£
Higher of:	Annual value = £6,000, or	6,000
	Rent paid by employer = (£450 × 12) = £5,400	
Less: Rent paid by Eve (£100 × 12)		(1,200)
Assessable benefit – 2013/14		4,800

(e) True or false

	True	False
Furniture provided by an employer is taxed at 25% of the market value per annum.		✓
Provision of workplace child care is an exempt benefit.	✓	
Loans of up to £6,000 provided to employees in order that they can buy items wholly, exclusively and necessarily for their employment are exempt from income tax	✓	
Reimbursement of expenses for home to work travel is tax allowable.		✓

Tutorial note

Furniture provided by an employer is taxed on the employee at 20% per annum of the market value when first made available to the employee.

Loans which do not exceed £5,000 at any time in the tax year or which are made to allow employees to purchase items wholly exclusively and necessarily for employment are an exempt benefit.

The expense relating to travel from home to work represents ordinary commuting and is not tax allowable.

8 BHARAT

(a) The answer is B.

Working

Use of asset benefit = (£3,600 × 20% × 6/12) = £360

Tutorial note

The benefit for the use of a company asset such as a home cinema system is 20% of the market value of the asset when first made available to the employee.

Bharat has only had use of the system for six months in the tax year 2013/14, therefore the benefit must be time apportioned.

(b) The answer is B.

(c) Job related accommodation

	Job related	**Not job related**
Accommodation provided for a school caretaker	✓	
Accommodation provided for the Prime Minister	✓	
Accommodation provided for a sales director so that he may entertain prospective customers		✓

Tutorial note

*Accommodation provided for a school caretaker and for the Prime Minister is job related as it is provided for the **better performance of their duties** and it is **customary** for such employments to be provided with accommodation.*

Accommodation supplied for directors can only be job related if special security considerations apply.

(d) The answer is £4,640.

Working

		£
Higher of:	Annual value = £5,600, or	5,600
	Rent paid by employer = (£420 × 12) = £5,040	
Less: Rent paid by Cyd (£80 × 12)		(960)
Assessable benefit – 2013/14		4,640

(e) The answer is C.

Tutorial note

Statements (iii) and (iv) are correct.

Furniture is a taxable benefit and is calculated based on the market value of the furniture when first made available to the employee.

Therefore, statements (i) and (ii) are incorrect.

9 NIKITA

(a) The answer is £420.

Working

Beneficial loan benefit = £28,000 × (4.00% – 1%) × 6/12 = £420

Tutorial note

Beneficial loan interest benefit is calculated as follows:

= Outstanding loan × the difference between the official rate of interest (4% in 2013/14) and the actual interest rate paid by the employee.

However, as the loan was provided six months into the tax year 2013/14, the benefit must be time apportioned as the rates of interest quoted are annual rates.

(b) The answer is B.

A standard figure of £3,000 applies for van benefit.

(c) P11D benefits

	P11D employee	**All employees**
Cash vouchers		✓
Additional benefit for accommodation costing over a certain limit		✓
Cars	✓	

(d) The answer is £14,350.

Working

	£
Annual value	5,000
Additional charge for 'expensive' accommodation:	
(£150,000 – £75,000) × 4.00%	3,000
Furniture (20% × £40,000)	8,000
Heating bills	750
	16,750
Less: Rent paid by Molly (£200 × 12)	(2,400)
Assessable benefit – 2013/14	14,350

(e) The answer is D.

Tutorial note

Statements (i) and (iv) are correct.

10 GIBBS

(a) The answer is D.

Working

	£
Annual value	6,500
Additional charge for 'expensive' accommodation:	
(£250,000 – £75,000) × 4.00%	7,000
	13,500
Less: Rent paid by House (£150 × 12)	(1,800)
Assessable benefit – 2013/14	11,700

Tutorial note

The accommodation was purchased by Gibbs's employers in May 2010 and Gibbs moved in on 20 December 2010.

The accommodation had therefore been owned by the employers for less than six years when Gibbs first moved in.

Accordingly, the expensive accommodation benefit must be calculated using the original cost of the house plus improvements up to the start of the tax year, and not the market value when Gibbs first moved in.

The improvements in June 2013 are not included in the calculations for 2013/14 benefit as they were incurred during the tax year, rather than before the start of the tax year.

The cost of the improvements will however be included in next year's benefit calculation.

(b) The answer is £6,100.

Working

	£
Furniture benefit (£20,000 × 20%)	4,000
Household expenses (Note)	2,100
Assessable benefit – 2013/14	6,100

Tutorial note

The cost of the double glazing is not an assessable benefit as it is capital expenditure.

(c) The answer is £400.

Working

	£
Payment under staff suggestion scheme – exempt	–
Telephone expenses	400
Assessable benefit – 2013/14	400

Tutorial note

Betsy earns below £8,500. However, this has no effect on the calculation of her benefit as payment of an employee's liabilities (i.e. the telephone bill) is taxable on all employees.

Payments made under a staff suggestion scheme are exempt benefits.

Telephone bills paid by the employer are assessable benefits valued at the cost to the employer.

(d) The answer is C.

Tutorial note

Provision of free or subsidised meals in a canteen is a tax free benefit provided there are canteen facilities for all staff.

11 EXEMPT BENEFITS

(a) £5,000

(b) £4

(c) £25

12 PERDITA

	Exempt	Not exempt
One mobile telephone per employee	✓	
Use of a pool car	✓	
Use of a van for a fortnight's camping holiday. There is no other private use.		✓
Provision of a car parking space in a multi-storey car park near the place of work	✓	
Childcare vouchers of £50 per week spent with an unapproved child minder		✓
Provision of bicycles for staff who have worked for the company for at least seven years		✓
Provision of an interest free loan of £4,000 made on 6 April 2013 and written off on 5 April 2014		
– provision of loan	✓	
– write off of loan		✓

Tutorial note

The van benefit is assessable unless the private use by the employee is incidental.

Childcare vouchers must be with an approved child minder to be an exempt benefit.

The provision of bicycles or cycling safety equipment to enable employees to get to and from work are exempt benefits but only provided they are available to staff generally. Therefore only being available to staff who have worked for the company for at least seven years would make the benefit taxable, not exempt.

Loans which total no more than £5,000 at any time in the tax year are exempt. However, loans of any amount which are written off will be an assessable benefit.

13 JOEY

(a) £8,500

(b) £Nil

(c) £5,000

Tutorial note

There is no assessable benefit on a pool car.

14 HAYLEY

(a) £5

(b) £150

(c) £8,000

15 HF LTD

(a) The answer is A.

Tutorial note

Provision of sport and recreational facilities open to staff but not the general public is an exempt benefit.

Payment of an employee's gym subscription of £450 would be taxed on the employee.

(b) £50

(c) 20

(d) 10

16 JADEJA PLC

	Exempt	**Not exempt**	**Partly exempt**
Free annual health screening which costs the employer £350 per head.	✓		
An annual staff party which costs £220 per head		✓ (i)	
Payments of £7 per night for personal expenses when employees have to stay away from home elsewhere in the UK		✓(ii)	
Removal expenses of £12,000 paid to an employee who had to relocate to a new town when she was promoted			✓(iii)
Childcare vouchers of £40 per week provided to employees earning between £50,000 and £100,000 per year			✓(iv)
A smart phone issued to all staff of manager grade	✓(v)		

Tutorial note

(i) *Staff parties are only exempt if they are no more than £150 per head.*

(ii) *Personal expense payments up to £5 per night in the UK are exempt, but if the payments exceed this limit they are taxable.*

(iii) *The first £8,000 of removal expenses are exempt.*

(iv) *Childcare vouchers up to £28 per week are tax free for higher rate taxpayers.*

(v) *Smart phones are exempt in the same way as mobile phones (i.e. one phone per employee)*

17 DHONI LTD

	Exempt	Taxable
Payment of £800 fees for office employees attending computer skills courses	✓	
Free tickets for all staff to attend a high profile athletics event sponsored by the employer. The tickets cost members of the public £25.	✓	
Long service awards of £500 cash for employees completing 20 years service		✓(Note i)
Private medical insurance for employees who work only in the UK		✓(Note ii)
A payment of £500 to an employee in accordance with the rules of the staff suggestion scheme.	✓	
Free eye tests for all staff working with computers	✓	

Tutorial note

(i) *In order to be exempt, long service awards must be no more than £50 for each year of service provided service is at least 20 years. The award must not be in cash and the recipient must not have had an award within the previous 10 years. A cash award would be taxable.*

(ii) *Private medical insurance is a taxable benefit unless it is for employees who are working outside the UK.*

INCOME FROM PROPERTY

18 GED

	TRUE	FALSE
Property losses from furnished lettings cannot be deducted from profits on unfurnished lettings.		✓
Ged and his wife occupy the same property. They can each have a rent a room exemption of £4,250.		✓
Income from property is taxed on an accruals basis.	✓	
Broad receives a salary of £25,000 and £3,000 rent from letting out a room in his house. He has no other rental income. He will not have to pay any tax on the rent.	✓	

Tutorial note

The first statement is false because net rental income is found by netting off all the rental profits and losses of the year, irrespective of whether the properties are furnished or unfurnished. The exception to this is in respect of furnished holiday accommodation where any losses can only be carried forward and deducted from future profits of the furnished holiday accommodation business.

The second statement is false because the rent a room limit is per property and so husband and wife cannot have an exemption each.

The third statement is true because property income is taxed on the basis of the rents that are due in the tax year and the expenses that are incurred, not when income is actually received or when expenses are paid.

The fourth statement is true because the rents will be covered by the rent a room exemption.

19 HOWARD

The answer is D.

Tutorial note

Wear and tear allowance is only given for furnished properties and the installation of a new central heating boiler would be a capital item.

20 GEORGIA

	One bedroom flat	*Four bedroom house*
	£	£
Income:		
(£500 × 9) + (£525 × 3)	6,075	
(£480 × 5)		2,400
Expenses:		
Insurance	(200)	
Repairs (£850 – £500) (Note)	(350)	
Gardening (£20 × 5)		(100)
Wear and tear allowance		
(10% × £6,075)	(608)	
Rental profit	4,917	2,300

Tutorial note

The new boiler is a capital item and its cost cannot be offset against the rental income on the flat.

Do not forget to calculate a wear and tear allowance on the flat as it is let furnished!

21 SHEILA

	Three bedroom house	*Two bedroom flat*
	£	£
Income:		
(£1,000 × 5) + (£1,000 × 4)	9,000	
Less: Bad debt relief	(1,000)	
	8,000	
(£600 × 9)		5,400
Expenses:		
Commission (£8,000 × 5%)	(400)	
Council tax and water rates		
(£1,250 × 11/12)		(1,146)
Insurance (£400 × 11/12)		(367)
Wear and tear allowance		
10% × (£5,400 – £1,146)		(425)
Rental profit	7,600	3,462

Tutorial note

Rental income is assessed on an accruals basis; therefore all of the rent accrued should be brought into the computation.

However, there is relief for the August rent which is irrecoverable. It can be deducted as a bad debt.

Note that in the CBT if there is a proforma already set up with narrative, and there is no bad debt relief expense, it is acceptable to just include in the rental income section the net rents actually received (i.e. £8,000 in this case) rather than two entries of rents accrued (£9,000) and the £1,000 bad debt deduction.

If there is part private use of a property by the owner, then expenses which cannot be directly attributed to the let period must be time apportioned to exclude the period of private use. Expenses relating wholly and exclusively to the period when the property is ***available for letting*** *are allowable, the property does not have to be actually let at that time. In this case the flat was occupied privately for 1 month so it was available for letting for 11 months and so only 11/12 of the council tax, water rates and insurance can be allowed.*

A wear and tear allowance is given for furnished properties.

The allowance available is:

10% × (Rent received – Water rates and council tax paid by the landlord)

Another way of putting this is to say:

10% × (Rent received – Expenses which are the responsibility of the tenant but which are paid by the landlord).

22 WILL

	Two bedroom cottage	*One bedroom flat*	*Three bedroom house*
	£	£	£
Income:			
(£500 × 12)	6,000		
(£3,600 × 9/12)		2,700	
Annual rent			4,300
Expenses:			
Gardening (£50 × 12)	(600)		
Cleaning (£70 × 12)	(840)		
Repairs	(400)		
Water rates		(500)	
Insurance – flat		(500)	
Insurance – house			
(£1,000 × 6/12) + (£1,200 6/12)			(1,100)
Wear and tear allowance			
(£6,000 × 10%)	(600)		
((£2,700 – 500) × 10%)		(220)	
Rental profit	3,560	1,480	3,200

Tutorial note

A wear and tear allowance is given for furnished properties.

The allowance available is:

10% × (Rent received – Water rates and council tax paid by the landlord)

23 EDWARD

	Four bedroom house	*Two bedroom bungalow*
	£	£
Income:		
(£7,200 × 10/12)	6,000	
Less: bad debt (£7,200 × 1/12)	(600)	
(£550 × 6)		3,300
Expenses		
Gardening	(500)	
Council tax		(1,100)
Repairs		(150)
Wear and tear allowance		
(£3,300 – £1,100) × 10%		(220)
Rental profit	4,900	1,830

Tutorial note

Rental income is assessed on an accruals basis; therefore all of the rent accrued should be brought into the computation.

However, there is relief for the rent which is irrecoverable. It can be deducted as a bad debt.

Note that in the CBT if there is a proforma already set up with narrative, and there is no bad debt relief expense, it is acceptable to just include in the rental income section the net rents actually received (i.e. £5,400 in this case) rather than two entries of rents accrued (£6,000) and the £600 bad debt deduction.

The cost of fitting a new kitchen is disallowed as a capital cost.

Wear and tear allowance is based on 10% of the net of the rents of £3,300 less the water rates and council tax paid by the landlord of £1,100.

24 REBECCA

	15 Olden Way	*29 Harrow Crescent*	*42 Long Close*
	£	£	£
Income:			
(£600 × 12 months)	7,200		
(£500 × 6 months)		3,000	
(£750 × 5 months)			3,750
Expenses:			
Insurance			
(£150 × 9/12 + £180 × 3/12)	(158)		
(£120 × 9/12 + £140 × 3/12)		(125)	
(£160 × 8/12)			(107)
Water rates	(80)	(100)	(85)
Wear and tear allowance:			
10% (£7,200 – £80)	(712)		
10% (£3,000 – £100)		(290)	
10% (£3,750 – £85)			(367)
Rental profit	6,250	2, 485	3,191

Tutorial note

*Expenses are allowable on an accruals basis; therefore the insurance **accrued** in the tax year should be brought into the computation. It is therefore necessary to time apportion the expense.*

A wear and tear allowance is given for furnished properties.

The allowance available is:

10% × (Rent received – Water rates and council tax paid by the landlord).

25 WINSTON

(a) The answer is £4,250.

Tutorial note

A taxpayer can receive up to £4,250 of rents tax free for renting out a room in their only or main residence.

(b) The answer is no.

Tutorial note

The rent a room limit applies to gross rents before expenses.

(c) The answer is no.

Tutorial note

The rent a room limit applies to the property not each individual lodger.

(d) The answer is no.

Tutorial note

Rent a room only applies to furnished lettings.

26 BOB

(a) The answer is £Nil.

Tutorial note

Bob's total rents for the year are £3,640 (£70 × 52). This is less than the rent a room limit of £4,250 so the rents are exempt.

(b) The answer is £18,000.

Working

Barry's rents exceed the rent a room limit of £4,250.

Using normal rental income rules his net rental profit is:

	£
Rent (£2,000 × 12 months)	24,000
Less: Expenses (£300 × 12 months)	(3,600)
Wear and tear allowance (£24,000 × 10%)	(2,400)
Property income	18,000

Using the rent a room method, Barry ignores his actual expenses and simply deducts £4,250 from his gross rents as follows:

	£
Rent (£2,000 × 12 months)	24,000
Less: Rent a room relief	(4,250)
Property income	19,750

The normal property income rules give a lower assessable amount and therefore "rent-a-room relief" will not be claimed.

(c) The statement is true.

Tutorial note

The rent a room relief only applies automatically if the rents do not exceed £4,250.

27 WEAR AND TEAR ALLOWANCE

(a) The answer is C and D are both true.

(b) The statement is false.

Tutorial note

Property income losses can only be offset against an individual's property income profits.

(c) The statement is true.

Tutorial note

Capital costs such as improvements are not deductible from rents.

28 ROSALIE

(a) The answer is £2,070.

Working

Insurance expense = (£1,800 × 3/12) + (£2,160 × 9/12) = £2,070

(b) The answer is B.

Tutorial note

All the other statements are true.

(c) The statement is true.

Tutorial note

Losses made on renting out a property can only be offset against property profits.

(d) The statement is false.

Tutorial note

Property losses which cannot be offset in the year they are incurred can be carried forward against future property income profits.

29 LAURIE

	Yes	No
Can I use the rent a room exemption for letting my country cottage?		✓
If I let the property out for 17 weeks out of the 35 weeks it is available, can I claim to treat it as a furnished holiday letting?	✓	
If the cottage is classed as furnished holiday accommodation and the letting makes a loss, do I have to carry the loss forward against future rental profits in respect of furnished holiday accommodation?	✓	

Tutorial note

Rent a room relief is only available for letting a room in a taxpayer's own residence.

Furnished holiday letting rules can apply provided:

(i) The property is situated in the UK or an EEA country.

(ii) It is let furnished.

(iii) The letting is on a commercial basis with a view to the realisation of profits.

(iv) It is available for commercial letting, to the public generally, as holiday accommodation for not less than 210 days a year.

(v) The accommodation is actually let for at least 105 days a year.

The advantages of having a letting classed as furnished holiday letting

(i) The profits are treated as relevant earnings for the purposes of relief for personal pension scheme contributions.

(ii) Capital gains tax rollover relief and Entrepreneurs' relief is available. These reliefs are not examined in the personal tax assessment.

(iii) Capital allowances can be claimed instead of the 10% wear and tear allowance.

If Laurie makes a loss on letting his holiday cottage, the loss must be carried forward and deducted from future profits of the furnished holiday accommodation business.

INVESTMENT INCOME

30 PATRICIA

(a) The answer is Nil.

Tutorial note

ISA interest is exempt and NS&I interest is paid gross.

(b) Investment income

Received gross	Received net
Interest on 3½% War Loan (government stock) Interest from NS&I bank accounts	Bank deposit interest Building society interest Interest on unquoted loan notes in a UK company

(c) The answer is B.

Working

Ian's gross dividend = (£326 × 100/90) = £362.22

This will be taxed at 32.5% but a 10% tax credit can be deducted.

Additional tax due from Ian = £362.22 × (32.5% – 10%) = £81.50

(d) The statement is false as dividend tax credits cannot be repaid.

Tutorial note

Dividends are received net of a 10% tax credit. The must be grossed up for inclusion in the income tax computation at 100/90.

They are taxed at the following rates:

- *10% if falling in the basic rate band*
- *32.5% if falling in the higher rate band.*

The 10% tax credit can be deducted but cannot be repaid.

So, a taxpayer who only received dividend income will never receive a tax repayment. However, other tax paid by a taxpayer on other sources of income can lead to a repayment.

31 RAVI

(a) The maximum amount that Ravi can invest in an ISA during 2013/14 is £11,520

Tutorial note

The maximum that an individual aged 18 or over can invest in an ISA in 2013/14 is £11,520.

However, the maximum that can be invested in a cash ISA is £5,760.

Therefore if the maximum £11,520 is invested, it must be invested wholly or partly in a stocks and shares ISA.

Note that those aged 16 and over can invest in a cash ISA, however only those aged 18 or over can invest in a stocks and shares ISA.

(b) The statement is true.

Tutorial note

Gambling winnings are not subject to income tax.

(c) £50

	£
Interest	11,000
Less: Personal allowance (age 68)	(10,500)
Taxable income	500
Tax at 10%	50

Tutorial note

Interest falling in the first £2,790 of taxable income is taxed at 10%. The interest is received gross so there is no tax deducted at source.

32 HANNAH

(a) National lottery winnings

NS&I Savings Certificate interest

These are both exempt sources.

(b) The answer is C.

Tutorial note

The ISA interest is exempt.

The bank account interest is received net of tax so must be grossed up at 100/80 to give the gross taxable amount. This is £1,075 (£860 × 100/80).

33 CASTILAS

(a) The answer is B.

Tutorial note

The dividend will fall wholly in the basic rate band and will be taxed at 10%.

(b) The answer is D.

Tutorial note

The tax credit on dividends is not repayable.

34 JAL

(a) Investment income

Received net	Received gross	Exempt
Interest on a building society account Interest on Sketch Ltd unquoted loan notes	Interest on Treasury Stock	Interest on ISAs Interest on NS&I Savings Certificates Premium bond winnings

(b) The answer is A.

Both these sources are received net of tax of 20%.

Income tax = (£120 + £160) × 20/80 = £70

Tutorial note

Income received net of 20% tax must be included in the tax computation gross. The net income must be multiplied by 100/80 to give the gross taxable amount.

In this question you were asked to find the tax credits related to this interest which means the tax deducted before Jal received the interest.

This can be found by multiplying the gross amount by 20% or (as here) the net amount by 20/80.

35 NAOMI

(a) The tax credit is £31.11 (£280 × 10/90).

(b) The gross dividend is £311 (£280 × 100/90).

36 THERESE

	True	False
If Therese has winnings from Premium Bonds they must be declared on her tax return.		✓
If the tax liability of an individual who has dividend income only is less than the tax credit on the dividends, then a repayment can be claimed.		✓

Tutorial note

Premium bonds winnings are exempt from tax and therefore do not need to be included on the tax return.

The tax credit on dividends is not repayable.

37 KIRA

	Yes	No
Profit on disposal of an asset		✓
Rental profits	✓	
Tips earned whilst working in a bar	✓	
Damages for injury at work		✓

Tutorial note

The profit on the disposal of an asset is liable to capital gains tax, not income tax.

Compensation received for injury or death is tax free.

Rental income is subject to income tax, as is employment income, including tips.

38 GINNY

(a) Investment income

Exempt from income tax	Taxable
Interest from National Savings Certificates Interest from Individual Savings Accounts	Interest from building society accounts Interest from bank accounts NS&I Direct Saver Account Interest Interest from Gilts (Government stocks)

(b) The answer is C

Tutorial note

Interest on quoted loan notes is received gross.

Bank interest is received net.

Therefore, the gross total is £610 (£160 + (£360 × 100/80)).

(c) Hermione receives a dividend of £243 in December 2013.

What is the tax credit attached to this dividend? £.........*27 (W1)*............

What is the gross amount of the dividend? £......*270 (W2)*............

Workings

(W1) Tax credit = (£243 × 10/90) = £27

(W2) Gross dividend = (£243 × 100/90) = £270

39 TARAN

(a) In 2011/12 the maximum amount that Taran (aged 42) can invest in a cash ISA is £...***5,760***...........

(b) The statement is true.

(c) The statement is true.

Tutorial note

Income received from an ISA is exempt.

Gains realised on disposal of stocks and shares in an ISA are exempt from capital gains tax.

40 LANG

The answer is B.

Tutorial note

The first statement is correct.

Statement (ii) is incorrect as all the NS&I interest is taxable.

Statement (iii) is incorrect as the repayment would be £85 (£340 × 20/80) tax deducted from the building society interest. The NS&I interest is paid gross and has no tax deducted.

41 HUANG

The answer is A.

Working:

Income tax computation – 2013/14

	£
Dividends (£10,800 × 100/90)	12,000
Less: Personal allowance	(9,440)
Taxable income (all dividends)	2,560
Income tax liability:	
£2,560 × 10% (Dividends)	256.00

Tutorial note

Dividends from shares in an ISA are exempt.

COMPUTATION OF TOTAL AND TAXABLE INCOME

42 JESSICA

(a) The tax year runs from 6 April 2013 to 5 April 2014 and Jessica's salary changes after one month of this period. The salary must therefore be time apportioned to find the amount received in the tax year.

Taxable salary for 2013/14 = (£36,300 × 1/12) + (£20,000 × 11/12) = £21,358.

(b) The bonus for 2013/14 is £2,300.

This is the bonus paid in 2013/14.

The accounting year to which it relates is not relevant.

(c) The commission received in 2013/14 is £1,602 (£21,358 × 7.5%).

43 JANE

(a) The answer is £19,500

The tax year runs from 6 April 2013 to 5 April 2014 and Jane's salary changes after three months of this period. The salary must therefore be time apportioned to find the amount received in the tax year.

Taxable salary for 2013/14 = (£18,000 × 3/12) + (£20,000 × 9/12) = £19,500

(b) The answer is £1,000.

The bonus taxable in 2013/14 is the one received during 2013/14.

(c) The commission taxable for 2013/14 is the amount received in the year of £1,170 (£19,500 × 6%).

44 EFFIE

The answer is B.

	£
Salary (£30,000 × 6/12 + £33,600 × 6/12)	31,800
Reimbursed expenses (see note)	Nil
Less: Payroll giving contribution	(480)
Taxable employment income	31,320

Tutorial note

The tax year runs from 6 April 2013 to 5 April 2014 and Effie's salary changes after six months of this period. The salary must therefore be time apportioned to find the amount received in the tax year.

The contribution to charity under the payroll giving scheme is an allowable deduction from employment income.

However, a Gift Aid donation is not deducted from employment income. Relief is available for the donation, but not as an allowable deduction from employment income.

Instead, basic rate relief is given at source as payments to the charity are paid net of 20% tax. Higher rate and additional rate relief is given by extending the basic rate band and higher rate band by the gross Gift Aid donation.

Normally reimbursed employment expenses are included as part of employment income. The employee then has to make a claim to deduct the allowable expenses from their employment income. If the employer has a dispensation in respect of these expenses then the employer does not have to report the expenses and the employee does not have to make a claim. The expenses can be ignored.

45 HARRY

(a) Harry's taxable salary for 2013/14 is £16,500 (£1,300 × 9) + (£1,600 × 3).

Tutorial note

The tax year runs from 6 April 2013 to 5 April 2014 and Harry's salary changes after nine months of this period. The salary must therefore be time apportioned to find the amount received in the tax year.

(b) Harry's taxable bonus for 2013/14 is £1,125 paid to him on 15 April 2013.

46 MANINDER

The answer is C.

	£
Salary	25,000
Round sum expense allowance	12,000
	37,000
Less: Allowable deductions	
Pension contribution (£25,000 × 5%)	(1,250)
Payroll giving (£20 × 12)	(240)
Round sum allowance	
(amount spent on business travel and subsistence) (70%)	(8,400)
Assessable employment income	27,110

Tutorial note

A round sum allowance is included as taxable employment income, but a deduction can be made for all business expenses incurred except for amounts spent on entertaining.

47 SALLY

(a) The answer is C.

	£
Allowable under HMRC rules:	
10,000 × 45p	4,500
10,000 × 25p	2,500
	7,000
Less: Received (20,000 × 25p)	(5,000)
Allowable employment income expense	2,000

(b) The answer is A.

Tutorial note

Contributions to an occupational pension scheme are paid gross and deducted from earnings for tax purposes.

Pension contributions made by an employer are an exempt benefit.

(c) The answer is C.

Tutorial note

When an employee receives a round sum allowance for expenses, they are taxed on the allowance received less what they spend on business expenses EXCEPT entertaining customers/potential customers.

(d) The answer is C.

Tutorial note

The question asks which statement is ALWAYS true.

The options A and B may or may not be true. Option D is not true.

48 BERNIE

	True	False
Bernie cannot contribute to both a personal pension scheme and to his employer's occupational scheme.		✓
Personal pension scheme payments are made net of 10% tax.		✓
Relief for occupational pension payments is given by deducting the payments made from gross earnings.	✓	
Gary pays a cheque for £260 to his personal pension scheme. He will obtain tax relief by extending his basic rate band by £260.		✓
Sobia is currently unemployed and has no earnings. She cannot contribute to a personal pension scheme because she has no relevant earnings.		✓
Pension contributions made by an employer on behalf of an employee are an assessable benefit.		✓

Tutorial note

Gary will pay his personal pension contribution net of 20% tax. He can use the grossed up amount of £325 (£260 × 100/80) to increase the threshold for higher rate and additional rate tax purposes.

Sobia can contribute up to £3,600 (gross amount) to her personal pension scheme even if she has no earnings.

Contributions made by an employer are an exempt benefit.

49 MICHELLE

	True	False
Michelle is employed as a tax consultant. She pays £520 per annum in subscriptions. £380 is paid to the Chartered Institute of Taxation and £140 to a local health club where Michelle often meets clients. Both subscriptions can be deducted from her employment income for tax purposes.		✓
In order for employment expenses to be deductible from employment income, they must be incurred wholly, exclusively and naturally in the performance of the employment.		✓
An employee spends £35 on taking a client out for lunch. His employer reimburses him for this amount. The employee will not have to pay tax on the £35 received.	✓	

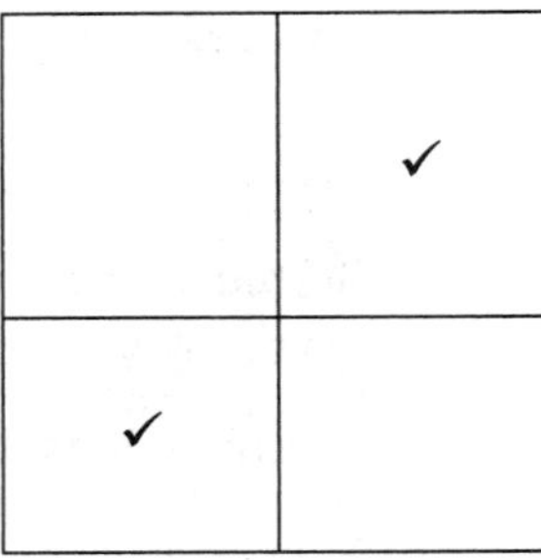

Sam is an accountancy trainee employed by a firm of accountants. He has to travel 10 miles per day to get to and from his place of employment. He can claim the costs of travelling as a deduction from his employment income for tax purposes.		✓
Cook pays £10 per month to Oxfam (an international charity) through the payroll giving scheme. This is a tax allowable deduction from his gross salary.	✓	

Tutorial note

Subscriptions to the CIOT are allowable for tax purposes. However, subscriptions to a local health club are not allowable, despite Michelle using the club to meet clients.

Expenses must be incurred wholly, exclusively and ***necessarily*** *in order to be allowable deductions from employment income.*

Subscriptions to a health club and travel from home to work do not pass this test.

An allowance for entertaining clients is a taxable benefit; however it can be deducted as an allowable expense if incurred wholly, exclusively and necessarily in the performance of duties. The net effect on employment income is therefore £Nil.

50 RON

(a) The answer is C.

	£
Allowable under HMRC rules:	
10,000 × 45p	4,500
8,000 × 25p	2,000
	6,500
Less: Received (18,000 × 38p)	(6,840)
Taxable employment income	340

(b) The answer is D.

Tutorial note

Political donations are not tax allowable.

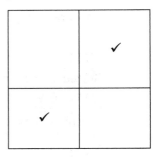

(c) The answer is B.

Tutorial note

Occupational pension scheme contributions are paid gross and deducted from employment income.

Employer contributions to pension schemes are not an assessable benefit.

(d) (i) £3,600

(ii) 100%

51 ASIF

(a) The answer is C.

Tutorial note

Payroll giving donations are tax deductible. Gift Aid donations are not allowable deductions from employment income.

Relief for Gift Aid donations is available by giving basic rate relief at source and by extending the basic rate and higher rate bands.

(b) The answer is D.

Tutorial note

Statement (ii) is incorrect because personal pension contributions are not deducted from income. Instead, relief is available by giving basic rate relief at source and by extending the basic rate and higher rate bands.

*Statement (v) is incorrect because the maximum pension contribution is the **higher** of £3,600 and 100% of earnings.*

(c) The answer is B.

	£
Allowable under HMRC rules:	
10,000 × 45p	4,500
4,000 × 25p	1,000
	5,500
Less: Received (20,000 × 28p)	(5,600)
Taxable employment income	100

Tutorial note

Home to work travel is not business travel and therefore not allowable under the HMRC rules.

52 ARKAN

	£
Salary	91,350
Personal pension scheme	0
Bonus	5,000
Car benefit	5,500
Dividend	11,000
Building society interest	750
Interest from ISA	0
Personal allowance	5,495
Taxable income	108,105

Workings

(W1) **Taxable income**

	£
Salary (£90,000 × 6/12) + (£90,000 × 1.03 × 6/12)	91,350
Personal pension scheme (not an allowable deduction)	0
Bonus	5,000
Car benefit	5,500
Dividend (£9,900 × 100/90)	11,000
Building society interest (£600 × 100/80)	750
Interest from ISA (exempt)	0
Total income	113,600
Personal allowance (W2)	(5,495)
Taxable income	108,105

(W2) **Personal allowance**

	£	£
Personal allowance		9,440
Net income (= Total income)	113,600	
Less: Gross personal pension contribution		
(£91,350 × 5% × 100/80)	(5,709)	
Adjusted net income	107,891	
Less: Limit	(100,000)	
Excess	7891 × 50%	(3,945)
Adjusted PA		5,495

53 PHLOX

	£
Pension	15,075
Dividend from Enterprise plc	5,000
ISA dividend	0
Building society interest	7,500
NS& I bank interest	805
Gift Aid payment	0
Gain on shares	0
Personal allowance	9,770
Taxable income	18,610

Workings

(W1) **Taxable income**

	£
Pension (£15,000 × 9/12) + (£15,000 × 1.02 × 3/12)	15,075
Dividend from Enterprise) (£4,500 × 100/90)	5,000
ISA dividend (exempt)	0
Building society interest (£6,000 × 100/80)	7,500
NS& I bank interest (received gross)	805
Gift Aid payment (not an allowable deduction)	0
Gain on shares (capital not revenue)	0
Total income	28,380
Personal allowance (W2)	(9,770)
Taxable income	18,610

(W2) **Personal allowance**

	£	£
Personal allowance (born before 6.4.1938)		10,660
Net income (= Total income)	28,380	
Less: Gross Gift Aid		
(£400 × 100/80)	(500)	
Adjusted net income	27,880	
Less: Limit	(26,100)	
Excess	1,780 × 50%	(890)
		9,770

54 ALEXIS

	£
Salary	41,167
Commission	1,200
Contribution to employer pension scheme	2,058
Employer's pension contribution	0
Mileage allowance – taxable amount	0
Mileage allowance – tax allowable expense	100
Dividend	1,000
Building society interest	437
Interest from ISA	0
Personal allowance	9440
Taxable income	32,206

Workings

(W1) **Taxable income**

	£
Salary (£40,000 × 5/12) + (£42,000 × 7/12)	41,167
Commission (1% × £120,000) paid 1 May 2013	1,200
Contribution to employer pension scheme (£41,167 × 5%)	(2,058)
Employer's pension contribution (exempt benefit)	0
Mileage allowance (W2) – expense	(100)
Dividend (£900 × 100/90)	1,000
Building society interest (£350 × 100/80)	437
Interest from ISA – exempt	0
Total income	41,646
Personal allowance	(9,440)
Taxable income	32,206

(W2) **Mileage allowance**

	£
Allowable under HMRC rules	
10,000 × 40p	4,000
4,000 × 25p	1,000
	5,000
Mileage allowance received (14,000 × 35p)	(4,900)
Allowable expense	100

55 DOMINIC

Dominic will pay £3,150 (£45,000 × 7%) into the scheme. This will be grossed up at 100/80 to give a gross contribution of £3,938. This amount can affect tax liability in two ways:

1 The grossed up amount reduces net income for the purposes of calculating restrictions on the personal allowance for taxpayers born before 6.4.1948 or with income over £100,000. This does not affect Dominic in 2013/14.

2 The grossed up amount extends the basic rate band so that less income is taxed in the higher rate band and more in the basic rate band.

Dominic has taxable income of £35,560 (£45,000 – £9,440). Before making the pension contribution £3,550 (£35,560 – £32,010) of this income is taxed in the higher rate band. The effect of the contribution of £3,938 is that all of his income will now be taxed at the basic rate of 20% rather than the higher rate of 40% saving him £710 (£3,550 × 20%).

The net after tax cost to Dominic of making the payment is £2,440 (£3,150 – £710).

COMPUTATION OF TAX PAYABLE AND PAYMENT OF TAX

56 ROGER

Income tax computation – 2013/14

	Total	*Other*	*Savings*	*Dividends*
	£	£	£	£
Pension	24,050	24,050		
Property income	3,000	3,000		
Dividends (£1,030 × 100/90)	1,144			1,144
Net income	28,194	27,050		1,144
Less: PAA (W)	(9,613)	(9,613)		
Taxable income	18,581	17,437	Nil	1,144

			£
Income tax:			
Other income	17,437	at 20%	3,487.40
Dividends	1,144	at 10%	114.40
	18,581		
Income tax liability			3,601.80

***Working:* Personal age allowance**

	£		£
Age allowance (born 6.4.38)			10,660
Net income = adjusted net income	28,194		
Less: Limit	(26,100)		
Excess	2,094	× 50%	(1,047)
Personal age allowance			9,613

Tutorial note

Roger was born before 6 April 1938 and so is over 75 at 6 April 2013. He is entitled to the higher personal age allowance. However, due to the level of his adjusted net income, the allowance has to be abated.

Adjusted net income = Net income less gross Gift Aid donations and gross Personal Pension contributions.

As Roger has not made any such payments, his Net income = his Adjusted net income.

Note that Roger's pension income is taxable income and is treated as earned "other income".

Key answer tips

It is important when using this type of layout to analyse the taxable income into "other income", "savings" and "dividends" as different rates of tax apply to the different sources of income.

Note that:

- the above layout should be possible if the CBT gives at least four columns to complete the calculation
- the total lines do not have to be inserted in the real CBT
- you may find it useful to do the computation on paper first before inputting on screen
- if the source of income is not specified in the CBT, always assume it is "other income"
- it is acceptable to have the total column at the end rather than the beginning if you prefer. However, we recommend that the analysis columns are in the fixed order: "other income", "savings" and then "dividends", as this is the order in which they must be taxed through the bands. Nil columns are not required.

57 RAY

Income tax computation – 2013/14

	Total		*Other*	*Dividends*
	£		£	£
Income	26,900		26,900	
Dividends (£900 × 100/90)	1,000			1,000
Net income	27,900		26,900	1,000
Less: PAA (W)	(9,850)		(9,850)	
Taxable income	18,050		17,050	1,000
Income tax:				
Other income	17,050	at 20%		3,410.00
Dividends	1,000	at 10%		100.00
	18,050			
Income tax liability				3,510.00

Key answer tips

If the source of the income is not specified, as in this case, always assume it is "other income".

***Working:* Personal age allowance**

	£		£
Age allowance			10,500
Net income	27,900		
Less: Gift Aid (£400 × 100/80)	(500)		
Adjusted net income	27,400		
Less: Limit	(26,100)		
Excess	1,300	× 50%	(650)
Personal age allowance			9,850

Tutorial note

Ray was born between 6 April 1938 and 5 April 1948 and is aged between 65 – 75 at 6 April 2013. He is entitled to the higher personal age allowance. However, due to the level of his adjusted net income, the allowance has to be abated.

Adjusted net income = Net income less gross Gift Aid donations and gross Personal Pension contributions.

Key answer tips

It is important when using this type of layout to analyse the taxable income into "other income", "savings" and "dividends" as different rates of tax apply to the different sources of income.

Note that:

- the above layout should be possible if the CBT gives at least four columns to complete the calculation
- the total lines do not have to be inserted in the real CBT
- you may find it useful to do the computation on paper first before inputting on screen
- it is acceptable to have the total column at the end rather than the beginning if you prefer. However, we recommend that the analysis columns are in the fixed order: "other income", "savings" and then "dividends", as this is the order in which they must be taxed through the bands.

58 JJ

Income tax computation – 2013/14

	Total	*Other*	*Savings*	*Dividends*
	£	£	£	£
Employment income	148,200	148,200		
BSI (£5,720 × 100/80)	7,150		7,150	
Dividends (£6,800 × 100/90)	7,556			7,556
Net income	162,906	148,200	7,150	7,556
Less: PA (Note)	(Nil)	(Nil)		
Taxable income	162,906	148,200	7,150	7,556

		£
Income tax:		
Other income	32,010 at 20%	6,402.00
Other income	116,190 at 40%	46,476.00
Savings	1,800 at 40%	720.00
	150,000	
Savings	5,350 at 45%	2,407.50
Dividends	7,556 at 37.5%	2,833.50
	162,906	
Income tax liability		58,839.00

Tutorial note

The personal allowance is reduced to £Nil as JJ has net income (and adjusted net income) of more than £118,880.

Adjusted net income = Net income less gross Gift Aid donations and gross Personal Pension contributions.

As JJ has not made any such payments, his Net income = his Adjusted net income.

Key answer tips

It is important when using this type of layout to analyse the taxable income into "other income", "savings" and "dividends" as different rates of tax apply to the different sources of income.

Note that:

- the above layout should be possible if the CBT gives five columns to complete the calculation
- the total lines do not have to be inserted in the real CBT
- you may find it useful to do the computation on paper first before inputting on screen
- it is acceptable to have the total column at the end rather than the beginning if you prefer. However, we recommend that the analysis columns are in the fixed order: "other income", "savings" and then "dividends", as this is the order in which they must be taxed through the bands.

59 BILL

Income tax computation – 2013/14

	Total	*Other*	*Savings*
	£	£	£
Employment income	10,500	10,500	
BSI (£2,400 × 100/80)	3,000		3,000
Net income	13,500	10,500	3,000
Less: PA	(9,440)	(9,440)	
Taxable income	4,060	1,060	3,000

Income tax:		
Other income	1,060 at 20%	212.00
Savings	1,730 at 10%	173.00
	2,790	
Savings	1,270 at 20%	254.00
	4,060	
Income tax liability		639.00
Less: Tax credits		
PAYE		(150.00)
BSI (£3,000 × 20%)		(600.00)
Income tax repayable		(111.00)

Tutorial note

Savings income falling into the first £2,790 of taxable income is taxed at 10%.

Here, the £2,790 band is partly used up by the £1,060 of other income. So the balance of the £2,790 band available is £1,730 (£2,790 – £1,060).

Key answer tips

It is important when using this type of layout to analyse the taxable income into "other income", "savings" and "dividends" as different rates of tax apply to the different sources of income.

Note that:

- the above layout should be possible provided the CBT gives four columns to complete the calculation
- the total lines do not have to be inserted in the real CBT
- you may find it useful to do the computation on paper first before inputting on screen
- it is acceptable to have the total column at the end rather than the beginning if you prefer. However, we recommend that the analysis columns are in the fixed order: "other income", "savings" and then "dividends", as this is the order in which they must be taxed through the bands.

If you are only provided with 3 columns then this layout will be appropriate

	Workings	*£*
Employment income		*10,500*
BSI	*(£2,400 × 100/80)*	*3,000*
Net income		*13,500*
Less: PA		*(9,440)*
Taxable income		*4,060*
Income tax:		
Other income		
(10,500 – 9,440)	*1,060 at 20%*	*212.00*
Savings	*1,730 at 10%*	*173.00*
	2,790	
Savings	*1,270 at 20%*	*254.00*
	4,060	
Income tax liability		*639.00*
Less: Tax credits		
PAYE		*(150.00)*
BSI	*(£3,000 × 20%)*	*(600.00)*
Income tax repayable		*(111.00)*

60 FENFANG

Income tax computation – 2013/14

	Total	*Other*	*Dividends*
	£	£	£
Employment income	70,000	70,000	
Dividends (£36,180 × 100/90)	40,200		40,200
Net income	110,200	70,000	40,200
Less: Adjusted PA (W1)	(5,690)	(5,690)	
Taxable income	104,510	64,310	40,200

			£
Income tax:			
Other income	34,710	at 20% (W2)	6,942.00
Other income	29,600	at 40%	11,840.00
	64,310		
Dividends	40,200	at 32.5%	13,065.00
	104,510		
Income tax liability			31,847.00
Less: Tax credits			
On dividends (£40,200 × 10%)			(4,020.00)
PAYE			(25,100.00)
Income tax payable			2,727.00

Workings

(W1) **Adjusted personal allowance**

	£		£
Personal allowance			9,440
Net income	110,200		
Less: PPC (£2,000 × 100/80)	(2,500)		
Gift Aid (£160 × 100/80)	(200)		
Adjusted net income	107,500		
Less: Limit	(100,000)		
Excess	7,500	× 50%	(3,750)
Adjusted PA			5,690

(W2) **Extended basic and additional rate bands**

	BR band	*AR band*
	£	£
Basic rate / Additional rate band	32,010	150,000
Plus: PPC (£2,000 × 100/80)	2,500	2,500
Gift Aid (£160 × 100/80)	200	200
Extended bands	34,710	152,700

Tutorial note

As Fenfang's adjusted net income exceeds £100,000, her personal allowance must be reduced.

Adjusted net income = Net income less gross Gift Aid donations and gross Personal Pension contributions.

As Fenfang has made both a Personal Pension payment and Gift Aid donation, her "adjusted net income" needs to be calculated and compared to the £100,000 limit.

In addition, her basic rate and additional rate bands need to be extended for the gross Personal Pension contribution and Gift Aid donation to decide the appropriate rate of tax to apply.

As her income falls below the extended £152,700 additional rate threshold, her income in excess of £34,710 is taxed at 40% (other income) and 32.5% (dividends).

Key answer tips

It is important when using this type of layout to analyse the taxable income into "other income", "savings" and "dividends" as different rates of tax apply to the different sources of income.

Note that:

- the above layout should be possible provided the CBT gives four columns to complete the calculation
- the total lines do not have to be inserted in the real CBT
- you may find it useful to do the computation on paper first before inputting on screen
- it is acceptable to have the total column at the end rather than the beginning if you prefer. However, we recommend that the analysis columns are in the fixed order: "other income", "savings" and then "dividends", as this is the order in which they must be taxed through the bands.

THEORY UNDERPINNING TOPIC AND PENALTIES

61 SADIE

Sadie,

I hope the following is helpful.

There are three potential issues here:

1 Amendments to a tax return can be made by a taxpayer up to 12 months after the filing date. For a 2012/13 return the filing date is 31 January 2014. You can therefore make an amendment to your return to include the rental income up to 31 January 2015.

After this date you still have to notify HMRC of any undeclared income and it is more likely that penalties will be charged.

2 Penalties for an incorrect tax return:

- There may be no penalty for this if HMRC consider this oversight to be a genuine mistake.
- If however, it is considered to be a failure to take reasonable care, a penalty of 30% of the tax lost could be incurred.

3 Payment of tax:

- If there is a tax liability, interest may be payable. This will be charged from the date the tax is due to the date it is paid. Outstanding tax should have been paid by 31 January 2014 so some interest will be due.
- There may also be a penalty for late payment on any unpaid tax.
- As any unpaid tax will be more than six months overdue, a penalty for late payment of 10% of the tax may be payable.

Kind regards

AAT student

Tutorial note

In addition to tax and possible interest, late payment penalties are applied to unpaid tax. However, late payment penalties only apply to the final payment of income tax, Class 4 NICs and capital gains tax.

The amount due is:

(i) 5% of the unpaid tax if it is more than 30 days late

(ii) A further 5% if more than six months late

(iii) A further 5% if more than 12 months late.

62 CHARLOTTE

Charlotte,

Here is the information you requested. I hope it is helpful.

Tax payments

Income tax is paid by two instalments, the first on the 31 January in the tax year (31 January 2014 for 2013/14) and the second on the 31 July after the tax year (31 July 2014 for 2013/14).

These are based on half of your prior year income tax payable.

No instalments are paid for capital gains tax.

Due on 31 January 2014

On 31 January 2015 you will have to pay the balance of any income tax due for 2013/14 and all of your 2013/14 capital gains tax. In your case this will be £6,230 which is your total liability of £14,230 less the £8,000 you have already paid by instalments.

In addition you will have to pay the first instalment of your 2014/15 income tax. This will be £4,665 as it is based on half of your 2013/14 income tax payable of £9,330.

This means that you must pay a total of £10,895 by 31 January 2015.

Consequences of late payment

If you pay tax late, then you are charged interest from the date you should have paid until the day before the tax is actually paid.

In addition, if you make your balancing payment of £6,230 late you may be charged a late payment penalty. If the payment is more than 30 days late a penalty of 5% of the tax due can be charged which increases if the tax is paid more than 6 months late.

Kind regards

AAT student

Tutorial note

In addition to tax and possible interest, late payment penalties are applied to unpaid tax. However, late payment penalties only apply to the final payment of income tax, Class 4 NICs and capital gains tax.

The amount due is:

(i) 5% of the unpaid tax if it is more than 30 days late

(ii) A further 5% if more than six months late

(iii) A further 5% if more than 12 months late.

63 KATIE

Katie

I have detailed the answers to your queries below.

Submission Dates

You can file your 2013/14 tax return online or file a paper return. Paper returns must be filed by 31 October 2014 and online returns by 31 January 2015.

For returns received less than 3 months before the filing date (in this case, after 31 October 2014) you have until 3 months after the date of issue.

Penalties for late submission

Penalties for submitting an individual's tax return late are as follows:

Within 3 months of the due date = £100 fixed penalty

Between 3 to 6 months of the due date = Daily penalties of £10 per day (Maximum 90 days so £900)

Between 6 to 12 months of due date = Additional 5% of tax due (Minimum £300)

More than 12 months after the due date = Additional 5% of tax due (Minimum £300)

More than 12 months after the due date if the taxpayer withholds information:

– deliberate and concealed = 100% of tax due (Minimum £300)

– deliberate and not concealed = 70% of tax due (Minimum £300)

Payment of tax

Income tax is paid by two instalments, the first on 31 January in the tax year (31 January 2014 for 2013/14) and the second on the 31 July after the tax year (31 July 2014 for 2013/14).

These are based on half of your prior year income tax payable.

Instalments are not due for 2013/14 as all your tax was collected by your employer in 2012/13. Instalments are not necessary in 2013/14 if more than 80% of your tax liability for the previous tax year (2012/13) was collected at source.

The balance of income tax is due on the 31 January after the tax year (31 January 2015).

Consequences of late payment

(i) Interest is charged, on a daily basis, from the date payment was due to the date paid

(ii) Penalties for late payment of tax are also due on the balancing payment (but not payments on account) and are calculated as follows:

- 5% of the unpaid tax if it is more than 30 days late
- A further 5% if more than six months late
- A further 5% if more than 12 months late.

If you have any further questions and queries please do not hesitate to contact me.

AAT student

Tutorial note

In addition to tax and possible interest, late payment penalties are applied to unpaid tax. However, late payment penalties only apply to the final payment of income tax, Class 4 NICs and capital gains tax.

64 CHARLIE

Dear Charlie,

Payments on account of your tax liability for any year must be paid by 31 January in that tax year, and by 31 July following the tax year. This is based on an estimate, using the preceding tax years' liability.

Therefore, when you made your tax payments on 31 January 2013 and 31 July 2013 for 2012/13, this was based on your liability for 2011/12.

When the final figures are sent to HMRC, if these two instalments are not enough to cover the full liability, a balancing payment is due on the 31 January following the tax year.

For 2013/14 your payments due will therefore be:

31 January 2014	(£8,600/2)	£4,300
31 July 2014	(£8,600/2)	£4,300
31 January 2015	(£9,000 – £8,600)	£400

I hope this makes things clearer. If you have any queries please do not hesitate to contact me.

Best regards

AAT Student

65 SOPHIA

There are several issues involved with not disclosing income to HMRC. Luckily this has not been going on for a long time so the consequences are not as bad as they could be.

1 Altering your 2012/13 tax return

Amendments to a tax return can be made by a taxpayer up to 12 months after the filing date. For a 2012/13 return the filing date is 31 January 2014. You can therefore make an amendment to your return to include the interest income and this should be done by 31 January 2015.

2 Penalty for incorrect return

As you have omitted some income from your tax return you have made an incorrect return. A penalty may be charged by HMRC and this varies according to whether they consider it to be a careless or deliberate error. A careless error can attract a penalty of up to 30% of the tax unpaid as a result of the error and a deliberate error a maximum penalty of 70% of unpaid tax.

The tax unpaid as a result of your error is £ 600 (40% of £1,500).

The penalties can be reduced if you disclose the income voluntarily before HMRC become aware of it. In your case it is likely that HMRC will treat this as a careless error and the maximum penalty they will charge is £ 180 (£600 × 30%) although this may be reduced to Nil due to your disclosure.

3 Late payment penalty and interest

As well as a penalty for an incorrect return, interest will be due on the unpaid tax from the date it should have been paid i.e. 31 January 2014.

A late payment penalty can also be charged. As the tax is between 6 and 12 months late this penalty could be 10% of the outstanding tax.

Best regards

AAT Student

Tutorial note

If the taxpayer files an incorrect tax return, a penalty equal to a percentage of the tax under declared may be charged. The penalty may be waived for inadvertent errors, as long as the taxpayer notifies HMRC of the error as soon as possible.

The percentage depends on the reason for the error.

Taxpayer behaviour	***Maximum penalty (% of tax lost)***
Mistake	*No penalty*
Failure to take reasonable care	*30%*
Deliberate understatement	*70%*
Deliberate understatement with concealment	*100%*

The penalties may be reduced at HMRC discretion, depending on the type of penalty and whether the taxpayer makes an unprompted disclosure of the error.

66 JOHNSON

The answer is D.

Both statements are false.

Tutorial note

Statement (i) only applies to paper returns, not all returns.

Statement (ii) is false because taxpayers can amend their returns up to 12 months, not 18 months, after 31 January following the end of the tax year.

67 ETHICAL RULES (1)

Key answer tips

Make sure you read written questions like this very carefully.

In part (a) the question is asking you which statement is NOT correct; it is very easy to misread and ignore the not.

(a) The answer is C.

The other three statements are correct.

Tutorial note

Whilst an accountant can be associated with returns that may omit information which would mislead HMRC, this is only true provided the information was not deliberately omitted and is more in the nature of supplementary information which would enhance understanding.

An accountant should not be associated with a return which has deliberately omitted sources of income or other information about taxable income.

(b) The answer is C.

Tutorial note

The accountant can only share information with the client, unless the client gives authority for others to be informed.

68 ETHICAL RULES (2)

(a) The answer is D.

The other three statements are correct.

Tutorial note

It is common practice for accountants to prepare tax returns for clients. However, the accountant can only prepare the return based on the information supplied by the client.

The client must always sign the return and the declaration included on the return, to confirm that they have supplied all relevant information.

It is the client's responsibility to submit a completed, signed form as his self assessment of his own tax position.

(b) The answer is C.

Tutorial note

An accountant generally needs the client's permission before revealing confidential information.

69 LAREDO

	True	False
HMRC does not send out a tax return to all individuals.	✓	
All tax records for an individual should be kept for at least 4 years.		✓
The maximum penalty for not keeping records is £2,000.		✓

Tutorial note

HMRC only sends tax returns to taxpayers with more complex tax affairs, such as directors or the self employed.

Tax records should be kept for 1 year from 31 January following the tax year for personal records and 5 years for property income records.

Taxpayers can be fined up to £3,000 for failure to keep records.

70 CLIENT ADVICE

(a) The answer is C.

The other three statements are correct.

Tutorial note

Tax evasion (such as deliberately failing to disclose all of your income) is illegal.

It is tax avoidance that uses legal means to reduce your tax bill.

(b) The answer is C.

71 NEW SOURCES OF INCOME

	True	False
An individual who does not normally receive a tax return is responsible for letting HMRC know if they have a new source of income.	✓	
Tax on chargeable gains is paid in two instalments on 31 January in the tax year and 31 July following the end of the tax year.		✓

Tutorial note

Notification to HMRC of the chargeability of a new source of income is required within six months of the end of the tax year in which the liability arises (i.e. by 5 October 2014 for 2013/14).

There are no instalments for capital gains tax.

All tax is due on 31 January following the end of the tax year (i.e. 31 January 2015 for the 2013/14 tax year).

72 AAT STUDENT

(a) The answer is B.

The other three statements are correct.

Tutorial note

The duty of confidentiality to the client applies in all circumstances to all individuals, except where there is suspicion of money laundering.

An accountant cannot therefore disclose information to anyone without the client's permission, including the client's spouse or civil partner.

(b) The answer is D.

Tutorial note

When money laundering is suspected an accountant should report his suspicions. This legal duty overrules the duty of confidentiality.

73 FILING DEADLINES

	True	False
The filing deadline for 2013/14 paper returns is 31 October 2014.	✓	
If you want to submit your 2013/14 tax return online, you must submit it by 31 January 2014.		✓

Key answer tips

The second statement is false because the filing date for 2013/14 returns is 31 January 20145, not 2014.

Another example which shows the need to read the question very carefully!

74 NASHEEN

	True	False
If a husband is ill, it is acceptable to discuss their tax affairs with their wife even if no letter of authorization exists.		✓
Accountants must follow the rules of confidentiality irrespective of the situation.		✓

Tutorial note

The first statement is false because the duty of confidentiality to the client applies in all circumstances to all individuals, except where there is suspicion of money laundering.

An accountant cannot therefore disclose information to anyone without the client's permission, including the client's spouse or civil partner.

The second statement is false because when money laundering is suspected an accountant should report his suspicions. This legal duty overrules the duty of confidentiality.

75 ZAHERA

	True	False
Barclay filed his 2012/13 tax return electronically on 20 March 2014. The return showed tax outstanding of £186. Barclay will be charged a late filing penalty of £100.	✓	
Caroli was due to pay a balancing payment of £4,200 on 31 January 2014. This was actually paid on 21 March 2014. Caroli will be charged interest from 31 January to 20 March.	✓	
If a return is filed late then a late filing penalty is always charged, even if a taxpayer has a reasonable excuse.		✓

Tutorial note

Penalties for submitting an individual's tax return late are as follows:

(i)	*Within 3 months of the due date*	*= £100 fixed penalty*
(ii)	*Between 3 to 6 months of the due date*	*= Daily penalties of £10 per day (Maximum 90 days)*
(iii)	*Between 6 to 12 months of due date*	*= Additional 5% of tax due (Minimum £300)*
(iv)	*More than 12 months after the due date*	*= Additional 5% of tax due (Minimum £300)*
(i)	*More than 12 months after the due date if the taxpayer withholds information:*	
	– deliberate and concealed	*= 100% (Minimum £300)*
	– deliberate and not concealed	*= 70% (Minimum £300)*

If a taxpayer has a reasonable excuse (e.g. serious illness or computer breakdown) then the late filing penalty may not be charged.

76 EMPLOYMENT STATUS

	Employment	Self employment
Contract for services is for		✓
Contract of service is for	✓	
A worker providing their own tools to perform the work would indicate		✓

Tutorial note

A self employed individual is contracted to perform a task, to produce an end result. He is contracted for his services provided.

However, an employee has a contract of service and is required to perform all tasks asked of him by his employer whilst in the service of the business that employs him.

Provision of own equipment is one of the factors HMRC will consider to decide the status of the individual, and indicates that the relationship is more likely to be that of self employment.

77 EMPLOYMENT OR SELF EMPLOYMENT (1)

	Employment	Self employment
Minimal degree of control exercised		✓
Being personally responsible for poor work		✓
Provision of sick and holiday pay	✓	
Being able to hire helpers		✓
Carrying out an engagement for a long period	✓	
Regular payment on a monthly basis	✓	

Key answer tips

You need to make sure that you know the factors that HMRC will consider in order to decide the status of an individual with regard to employment or self employment.

78 EMPLOYMENT OR SELF EMPLOYMENT (2)

	Employment	Self employment
Being able to refuse work		✓
Being committed to work a specified number of hours at fixed times	✓	
Being able to profit from sound management		✓
Having to carry out work yourself without being able to arrange for someone else to do it	✓	
Having to provide your own equipment		✓
Not taking any financial risk	✓	

Key answer tips

You need to make sure that you know the factors that HMRC will consider in order to decide the status of an individual with regard to employment or self employment.

79 TAX RETURN RESPONSIBILITY

The answer is C.

A taxpayer is ultimately responsible for ensuring that their tax return is accurately completed.

80 MINIMUM PENALTIES

Failure to keep records to support the tax return	£3,000
Being one month late in filing an income tax return	£100
Being 2 months late in paying a balancing payment of £4,000	£200 (5% × £4,000)

81 REASONABLE EXCUSE

The answer is D.

82 PENALTY TABLE

	Maximum penalty	**Minimum penalties**	
		Unprompted disclosure	**Prompted disclosure**
	% of tax lost	**% of tax lost**	**% of tax lost**
Failure to take reasonable care	30%	Nil	15%
Deliberate understatement	70%	20%	35%
Deliberate understatement with concealment	100%	30%	50%

TAX RETURNS

83 MELANIE

HM Revenue & Customs

Employment

Tax year 6 April 2013 to 5 April 2014

Your name: MELANIE

Your Unique Taxpayer Reference (UTR):

Complete an *Employment* page for each employment or directorship

1 Pay from this employment – the total from your P45 or P60 – *before tax was taken off*
£ 30000.00

2 UK tax taken off pay in box 1
£ 5146.00

3 Tips and other payments not on your P60 – *read the Employment notes*
£ .00

4 PAYE tax reference of your employer (on your P45/P60)
/

5 Your employer's name

6 If you were a company director, put 'X' in the box

7 And, if the company was a close company, put 'X' in the box

8 If you are a part-time teacher in England or Wales and are on the Repayment of Teachers' Loans Scheme for this employment, put 'X' in the box

Benefits from your employment – use your form P11D (or equivalent information)

9 Company cars and vans – *the total 'cash equivalent' amount*
£ 3000.00

10 Fuel for company cars and vans – *the total 'cash equivalent' amount*
£ .00

11 Private medical and dental insurance – *the total 'cash equivalent' amount*
£ 385.00

12 Vouchers, credit cards and excess mileage allowance
£ .00

13 Goods and other assets provided by your employer – *the total value or amount*
£ .00

14 Accommodation provided by your employer – *the total value or amount*
£ .00

15 Other benefits (including interest-free and low interest loans) – *the total 'cash equivalent' amount*
£ 900.00

16 Expenses payments received and balancing charges
£ .00

Employment expenses

17 Business travel and subsistence expenses
£ 200.00

18 Fixed deductions for expenses
£ .00

19 Professional fees and subscriptions
£ 250.00

20 Other expenses and capital allowances
£ .00

Shares schemes, employment lump sums, compensation, deductions and Seafarers' Earnings Deduction are on the *Additional information* pages enclosed in the tax return pack.

SA102 2013 Page E 1 HMRC 12/12

84 MICHAEL

HM Revenue & Customs

Capital gains summary

Tax year 6 April 2013 to 5 April 2014

1 Your name

MICHAEL

2 Your Unique Taxpayer Reference (UTR)

Summary of your enclosed computations

Please read the *Capital gains summary notes* on pages CGN 10 to CGN 13 before filling in this section. **You must enclose your computations, including details of each gain or loss, as well as filling in the boxes.**

3 Total gains *(Boxes 19 + 25 + 31 + 32)*

£ 14500.00

4 Gains qualifying for Entrepreneurs' Relief (but excluding gains deferred from before 23 June 2010) *- read the notes on page CGN 11*

£ .00

5 Gains invested under Seed Enterprise Investment Scheme and qualifying for exemption - *read the notes on page CGN 11 and 12*

£ .00

6 Total losses of the year - *enter '0' if there are none*

£ 20000.00

7 Losses brought forward and used in the year

£ 1600.00

8 Adjustment to Capital Gains Tax - *read the notes*

£ .00

9 Additional liability for non-resident or dual resident trusts

£ .00

10 Losses available to be carried forward to later years

£ 3100.00

11 Losses used against an earlier year's gain (special circumstances apply - *read the notes on page CGN 12)*

£ .00

12 Losses used against income - amount claimed against 2013–14 income - *read the notes on page CGN 13*

£ .00

13 Losses used against income - amount claimed against 2012–13 income - *read the notes on page CGN 13*

£ .00

14 Income losses of 2013–14 set against gains

£ .00

15 Deferred gains from before 23 June 2010 qualifying for Entrepreneurs' Relief

£ .00

Listed shares and securities

16 Number of disposals - *read the notes on page CGN 13*

3

17 Disposal proceeds

£ 42500.00

18 Allowable costs (including purchase price)

£ 30000.00

19 Gains in the year, before losses

£ 14500.00

20 If you are making any claim or election, put 'X' in the box

21 If your computations include any estimates or valuations, put 'X' in the box

SA108 2013 Page CG 1 HMRC 12/12

85 SULLIVAN

HM Revenue & Customs

Employment

Tax year 6 April 2013 to 5 April 2014

Your name: SULLIVAN

Your Unique Taxpayer Reference (UTR):

Complete an *Employment* page for each employment or directorship

1 Pay from this employment – the total from your P45 or P60 – *before tax was taken off*: £ 20000.00

2 UK tax taken off pay in box 1: £ 4200.00

3 Tips and other payments not on your P60 – *read the Employment notes*: £ .00

4 PAYE tax reference of your employer (on your P45/P60): /

5 Your employer's name: KHARRAL LTD

6 If you were a company director, put 'X' in the box:

7 And, if the company was a close company, put 'X' in the box:

8 If you are a part-time teacher in England or Wales and are on the Repayment of Teachers' Loans Scheme for this employment, put 'X' in the box:

Benefits from your employment – use your form P11D (or equivalent information)

9 Company cars and vans – *the total 'cash equivalent' amount*: £ 4000.00

10 Fuel for company cars and vans – *the total 'cash equivalent' amount*: £ 3500.00

11 Private medical and dental insurance – *the total 'cash equivalent' amount*: £ 600.00

12 Vouchers, credit cards and excess mileage allowance: £ .00

13 Goods and other assets provided by your employer – *the total value or amount*: £ 450.00

14 Accommodation provided by your employer – *the total value or amount*: £ .00

15 Other benefits (including interest-free and low interest loans) – *the total 'cash equivalent' amount*: £ 300.00

16 Expenses payments received and balancing charges: £ .00

Employment expenses

17 Business travel and subsistence expenses: £ .00

18 Fixed deductions for expenses: £ .00

19 Professional fees and subscriptions: £ .00

20 Other expenses and capital allowances: £ .00

Shares schemes, employment lump sums, compensation, deductions and Seafarers' Earnings Deduction are on the *Additional information* pages enclosed in the tax return pack.

SA102 2013 Page E 1 HMRC 12/12

Working

Box 13: Use of company camera = (£2,250 × 20%) = £450

86 GUILLE

Property income

Do not include furnished holiday lettings, Real Estate Investment Trust or Property Authorised Investment Funds dividends/distributions here.

20	Total rents and other income from property	£ 76320.00
21	Tax taken off any income in box 20	£ .00
22	Premiums for the grant of a lease – from box E on the Working Sheet – *read the notes*	£ .00
23	Reverse premiums and inducements	£ .00

Property expenses

24	Rent, rates, insurance, ground rents etc.	£ 9816.00
25	Property repairs, maintenance and renewals	£ 5000.00
26	Loan interest and other financial costs	£ .00
27	Legal, management and other professional fees	£ .00
28	Costs of services provided, including wages	£ 7300.00
29	Other allowable property expenses	£ .00

Calculating your taxable profit or loss

30	Private use adjustment – *read the notes*	£ .00
31	Balancing charges – *read the notes*	£ .00
32	Annual Investment Allowance	£ .00
33	Business Premises Renovation Allowance (Assisted Areas only) – *read the notes*	£ .00
34	All other capital allowances	£ .00
35	Landlord's Energy Saving Allowance	£ .00
36	10% wear and tear allowance – *for furnished residential accommodation only*	£ 7208.00
37	Rent a Room exempt amount	£ .00
38	Adjusted profit for the year – from box O on the Working Sheet – *read the notes*	£ 46996.00
39	Loss brought forward used against this year's profits	£ .00
40	Taxable profit for the year (box 38 minus box 39)	£ 46996.00
41	Adjusted loss for the year – from box O on the Working Sheet – *read the notes*	£ .00
42	Loss set off against 2013–14 total income – *this will be unusual – read the notes*	£ .00
43	Loss to carry forward to following year, including unused losses brought forward	£ .00

SA105 2013   Page UKP 2

Workings

Box 24: (£5,580 Insurance + £336 Water rates + £3,900 Council tax) = £9,816

Box 36: Wear and tear allowance = (£76,320 – £336 – £3,900) × 10% = £7,208

CHARGEABLE GAINS

BASICS OF CAPITAL GAINS TAX

87 CONNECTED PERSONS

For each statement, tick the appropriate box.

	Actual proceeds used	Deemed proceeds used	No gain no loss basis
(a) Sister gives an asset to her brother		✓	
(b) Civil partner gives an asset to civil partner			✓
(c) Luke sells an asset to his friend for £38,000. He later discovers the asset is worth £45,000.	✓		

Tutorial note

"Deemed proceeds used" is the term used in the specimen assessment provided by the AAT.

*The term means that the **market value of the asset** will be used instead of actual sale proceeds as the start point of the capital gain computation.*

Market value must be used where there is:

- *a disposal to a connected person (except for inter spouse and civil partnership transfers)*
- *a gift to any person*
- *sales at an undervaluation to anyone (except for inter spouse and civil partnership transfers)*

A sale at undervaluation is where an asset is deliberately / knowingly sold for less than the market value.

A bad bargain (i.e. accidentally selling for less than the asset is worth) will not be caught by special rules and the actual sale proceeds received would be used in this case.

Inter spouse and civil partnership transfers are always treated as nil gain / nil loss transactions.

88 HARRY AND BETSY

(a) The answer is C.

Working

	£
Proceeds	400,000
Less: Cost	(155,000)
Conservatory	(15,000)
Extension	(28,000)
Chargeable gain	202,000

(b) The answer is D

Working

	£
Proceeds	10,000
Less: Cost (part disposal)	
(£10,000/£10,000 + £25,000) × £15,000	(4,286)
Chargeable gain	5,714

Tutorial note

The cost of the chairs sold must be found by applying the part disposal formula to the cost:

Cost × A/A + B

Where A = gross sales proceeds, and
B = market value of the part of the asset kept.

(c) The statement is false.

Tutorial note

Auction costs are an allowable deduction from sales proceeds.

89 SAMANTHA

	Actual proceeds used	Deemed proceeds used	No gain no loss basis
(a) Samantha sells an asset to her colleague for £8,000. She then discovers that it was worth £10,000	✓		
(b) Neil sells an asset to his wife for £10,000 when the market value is £14,000			✓
(c) Simon gives an asset to his friend.		✓	

Tutorial note

"Deemed proceeds used" is the term used in the specimen assessment provided by the AAT.

The term means that the ***market value of the asset*** *will be used instead of actual sale proceeds as the start point of the capital gain computation.*

Market value must be used where there is:

- *a disposal to a connected person (except for inter spouse and civil partnership transfers)*
- *a gift to any person*
- *sales at an undervaluation to anyone (except for inter spouse and civil partnership transfers)*

A sale at undervaluation is where an asset is deliberately / knowingly sold for less than the market value.

A bad bargain (i.e. accidentally selling for less than the asset is worth) will not be caught by special rules and the actual sale proceeds received would be used in this case.

Inter spouse and civil partnership transfers are always treated as nil gain / nil loss transactions.

90 JAY AND CARLI

(a) The answer is £50,000.

	£
Proceeds	120,000
Less: Cost	(70,000)
Chargeable gain	50,000

Tutorial note

Repair costs are not capital expenditure and therefore not allowable deductions in the chargeable gains computation.

(b) The answer is a loss of £23,500.

	£
Proceeds	30,000
Less: Selling costs – auctioneers fees (£30,000 × 5%)	(1,500)
	28,500
Less: Cost	(50,000)
Purchase costs – auctioneer's fees (£50,000 × 4%)	(2,000)
Allowable capital loss	(23,500)

(c) The statement is false.

Tutorial note

Shares are not chattels, and so the sale of shares which cost and are sold for less than £6,000 is chargeable.

91 VICTORIA

The answer is B.

Tutorial note

Victoria is connected with her husband Cecil, son in law Mike, and her sister Janet.

92 JACOB

(a) The answer is A.

	£
Proceeds	300,000
Less: Cost	(180,000)
Enhancement expenditure	(60,000)
Chargeable gain	60,000

93 ESHE

The answer is D.

	£	£
Necklace		
Market value	50,000	
Less: Cost	(31,500)	
Chargeable gain		18,500
Table		
Proceeds	11,000	
Less: Cost	(8,000)	
Chargeable gain		3,000
Total chargeable gains		21,500
Less: Annual exempt amount		(10,900)
Taxable gains		10,600

Tutorial note

Disposals (i) and (ii) are to connected persons and so market value is automatically substituted for proceeds. The loss in disposal (ii) can only be deducted from future gains on disposals to her husband's brother so is ignored in the calculation of taxable gains.

Eshe is not connected to her cousin so market value would only be substituted if there was a deliberate sale at undervalue. This is not the case here so the actual proceeds of £11,000 are used.

94 KAMILAH

(a) The gain is £23,000 (£48,000 – £25,000).

Tutorial note

The destruction of an asset is a disposal with the insurance received as the proceeds figure.

(b) The answer is £14,107.

Working

	£
Proceeds	20,000
Less: Cost £20,000/(£20,000 + £36,000) × £16,500	(5,893)
Chargeable gain	14,107

Tutorial note

The cost of the acres sold must be found by applying the part disposal formula to the cost:

Cost × A/A + B

Where A = gross sales proceeds (i.e. before selling expenses)

and B = market value of the part of the asset kept

95 ALVIN

(a) **Disposal in June 2013**

	£
Proceeds (£83,000 + £2,000)	85,000
Less: Selling expenses	(2,000)
Net sales proceeds	83,000
Less: Cost £40,000 × £85,000/£85,000 + £110,000	(17,436)
Chargeable gain	65,564

Tutorial note

The cost of the acres sold must be found by applying the part disposal formula to the cost:

Cost × A/A + B

Where A = gross sales proceeds (i.e. before selling expenses)

and B = market value of the part of the asset kept

Questions involving part disposals of a number of acres of land are popular with examiners. It is important to apportion the cost of the part sold using the formula and NOT the number of acres sold.

The cost of the unsold land will be the remainder of the cost.

(b) **Disposal in December 2013**

	£
Proceeds	118,000
Less: Selling expenses	(1,500)
Net sales proceeds	116,500
Less: Cost (£40,000 – £17,436)	(22,564)
Chargeable gain	93,936

96 BEN

Asset	Sale proceeds	Cost	Gain/Loss
1	£5,000	£4,000	Exempt, as proceeds and cost are both < £6,000
2	£10,000	£7,000	£3,000, no special rules apply, as proceeds and cost are both > £6,000
3	£9,000	£3,000	The gain is £5,000. Gain is lower of: (£9,000 – £3,000) = £6,000, or 5/3 × (£9,000 – £6,000) = £5,000
4	£4,000	£9,000	Loss £3,000. Deemed proceeds of £6,000 must be used.

Tutorial note

The chattel marginal gain rules apply when the proceeds > £6,000 and the cost < £6,000.

The gain is taken to be the lower of

(i) The gain calculated as normal

(ii) 5/3 × (Gross proceeds – £6,000)

Special loss rules apply when proceeds < £6,000 and the cost > £6,000.

The allowable loss is calculated assuming gross sale proceeds of £6,000.

97 CHATTELS – MARGINAL GAIN

	Applies	Does not apply
A racehorse bought for £4,000 and sold for £7,500		✓
A necklace bought for £5,900 plus £200 of auction costs, and given away when its market value was £8,000		✓
An antique vase bought for £3,000 and sold for £8,200	✓	
A painting bought for £3,000 and sold for £5,900		✓
Shares bought for £2,100 and sold for £6,900		✓

Tutorial note

Marginal gain rules only apply when a non-wasting chattel is disposed of and the proceeds are > £6,000 and the cost < £6,000.

In this question this only applies to the vase.

The racehorse is a wasting chattel and exempt.

The necklace costs more than £6,000 and has disposal proceeds of more than £6,000.

The painting is exempt as the cost and proceeds are both below £6,000.

Shares are not chattels.

98 MATCHING STATEMENTS

Asset	Sale proceeds	Cost	Statement
1	£12,000	£18,000	(iii)
2	£5,000	£6,000	(i)
3	£8,000	£4,000	(v)
4	£7,000	£6,500	(ii)
5	£5,000	£7,000	(iv)

Statements:

(i) Exempt asset disposal

(ii) Calculate gain as normal

(iii) Calculate loss as normal

(iv) Sale proceeds deemed to be £6,000

(v) Marginal gain restriction applies

Tutorial note

Asset 2 cost exactly £6,000 and the proceeds are < £6,000.

The asset is therefore exempt as both the cost and sale proceeds are "less than or equal to" £6,000.

99 MARTOK

	Exempt	Not exempt
A bravery medal he inherited from his father.	✓	
A quarter share in a racehorse	✓	
Antique violin sold for £150,000		✓
His personal computer	✓	
Shares held in an ISA	✓	

Tutorial note

A decoration for valour acquired other than by purchase (i.e. inherited) is specifically an exempt asset for capital gains tax purposes.

A racehorse and personal computer are wasting chattels and therefore exempt.

Although shares are not exempt as chattels, shares held in an ISA are exempt from capital gains tax when sold.

TAXATION OF SHARES

100 STRINGER LTD

Chargeable gain calculation – 2013/14

	£
Proceeds (5,000 × £10)	50,000
Less: Cost (W)	(20,833)
Chargeable gain	29,167

***Working:* Share pool**

		Number	Cost
			£
July 2006	Purchase (8,000 × £8)	8,000	64,000
March 2007	Purchase (4,000 × £9)	4,000	36,000
		12,000	100,000
July 2009	Sale (£100,000 × 3,000/12,000)	(3,000)	(25,000)
		9,000	75,000
May 2013	Bonus issue (1 for 1)	9,000	Nil
		18,000	75,000
Feb 2014	Sale (£75,000 × 5,000/18,000)	(5,000)	(20,833)
Balance c/f		13,000	54,167

Key answer tips

Remember you are only being asked to calculate the gain on the February 2014 disposal. The July 2009 disposal is only important for the pool calculation.

You are also asked for the chargeable gain, not the taxable gain; therefore do not waste time deducting the annual exempt amount.

101 LULU LTD

Chargeable gain calculation

	£
Proceeds (8,000 × £7)	56,000
Less: Cost (W)	(29,538)
Chargeable gain	26,462

***Working:* Share pool**

		Number	Cost
			£
Oct 2004	Purchase (12,000 × £4)	12,000	48,000
June 2006	Bonus 1 for 12	1,000	Nil
		13,000	48,000
April 2010	Sale (£48,000 × 3,000/13,000)	(3,000)	(11,077)
		10,000	36,923
Jan 2014	Sale (£36,923 × 8,000/10,000)	(8,000)	(29,538)
Balance c/f		2,000	7,385

Key answer tips

Remember you are only being asked to calculate the gain on the January 2014 disposal. The April 2010 disposal is only important for the pool calculation.

You are also asked for the chargeable gain, not the taxable gain; therefore do not waste time deducting the annual exempt amount.

102 GILBERT LTD

Chargeable gain calculation

		£
(1)	On 2,200 shares matched with the 15 September purchase	
	Proceeds 2,200/8,000 × £65,000	17,875
	Cost	(20,000)
	Loss	(2,125)
(2)	On 5,800 shares matched with the pool	
	Proceeds (£65,000 – £17,875)	47,125
	Less: Cost (W)	(23,200)
	Chargeable gain	23,925
Total gain (£23,925 – £2,125)		21,800

***Working:* Share pool**

		Number	Cost £
May 2003	Purchase (8,000 × £4)	8,000	32,000
June 2007	Bonus 1 for 4	2,000	Nil
July 2009	Purchase (2,000 × £8)	2,000	16,000
		12,000	48,000
Sept 2013	Sale (£48,000 × 5,800/12,000)	(5,800)	(23,200)
Balance c/f		6,200	24,800

Tutorial note

In relation to individuals, we match shares disposed of in the following order:

- *first, with shares acquired on the same day as the disposal*
- *second, with shares acquired within the following 30 days (using the earliest acquisition first, i.e. on a FIFO basis)*
- *third, with the share pool (all the shares bought by the individual before the date of disposal).*

In this case there are 2,200 shares purchased on 15 September 2013 which is within 30 days after the disposal on 7 September 2013. Hence 2,200 of the shares sold on 7 September are matched with the purchase on 15 September.

The remaining 5,800 shares sold are matched with the share pool.

103 BELLA

Chargeable gain calculation

(1) On 1,000 shares matched with the 17 May 2013 purchase

	£
Proceeds (1,000 × £11)	11,000
Less: Cost (1,000 × £10)	(10,000)
Chargeable gain	1,000

(2) On pool shares

	£
Proceeds (8,000 × £11)	88,000
Less: Cost (W)	(46,222)
Chargeable gain	41,778

***Working:* Share pool**

		Number	*Cost* £
Sept 2006	Purchase (16,000 × £6)	16,000	96,000
June 2010	Rights issue 1 for 8 (2,000 × £4)	2,000	8,000
		18,000	104,000
May 2013	Sale (£104,000 × 8,000/18,000)	(8,000)	(46,222)
Balance c/f		10,000	57,778

Tutorial note

In relation to individuals, we match shares disposed of in the following order:

- *first, with shares acquired on the same day as the disposal*
- *second, with shares acquired within the following 30 days (using the earliest acquisition first, i.e. on a FIFO basis)*
- *third, with the share pool (all the shares bought by the individual before the date of disposal).*

In this case there are 1,000 shares purchased on 17 May 2013 which is within 30 days after the disposal on 14 May 2013. Hence 1,000 of the shares sold on 14 May are matched with the purchase on 17 May.

The remaining 8,000 shares sold are matched with the share pool.

104 BAJOR PLC

Chargeable gain calculation

	£
Proceeds	17,500
Less: Cost (W)	(9,035)
Chargeable gain	8,465

Working: **Share pool**

		Number	*Cost* £
Feb 2004	Purchase	2,000	7,560
July 2006	Bonus 1 for 10	200	Nil
Dec 2008	Purchase	500	2,800
		2,700	10,360
Apr 2010	Rights issue (I for 5) at £2.50	540	1,350
		3,240	11,710
Mar 2014	Sale (£11,710 × 2,500/3,240)	(2,500)	(9,035)
Balance c/f		740	2,675

CAPITAL GAINS TAX EXEMPTIONS, LOSSES, RELIEFS, TAX PAYABLE

105 GARIBALDI

	True	False
Brought forward capital losses cannot be used before current year capital losses.	✓	
Excess capital losses can be used against other income.		✓
Capital gains are taxed at 40% for higher rate taxpayers.		✓

Tutorial note

Current year losses must be set off before brought forward losses are considered.

Excess capital losses can only be carried forward and set against future net chargeable gains.

Higher rate taxpayers will pay capital gains tax at the rate of 28% for 2013/14.

106 JR

The answer is A

Working

Capital gains tax payable computation – 2013/14

	£	
Gross sale proceeds	25,620	
Less: Selling costs (2% × £25,320)	(512)	
Net sale proceeds	25,108	
Less: Cost	(8,500)	
Chargeable gain	16,608	
Less: Annual exempt amount	(10,900)	
Taxable gain	5,708	
Capital gains tax:		
£		
1,450 × 18% (W)		261.00
4,258 × 28%		1,192.24
5,708		
Capital gains tax payable		1,453.24

Remaining basic rate band

	£
Basic rate band	32,010
Less: Taxable income (£40,000 – £9,440)	(30,560)
Remaining basic rate band	1,450

Tutorial note

The taxable income falls below the basic rate band threshold, therefore there is some of the basic rate band remaining to match against the taxable gains.

Taxable gains fall partly into the remaining basic rate band and partly into the higher rate band. The capital gains tax liability is therefore calculated in two parts at 18% and 28%.

107 ANGELA

The answer is B.

Working

Capital gains tax computation – 2013/14	£
Sale proceeds	290,000
Less: Cost	(150,000)
Enhancement expenditure	(30,000)
Chargeable gain	110,000
Less: Annual exempt amount	(10,900)
Taxable gains	99,100
Capital gains tax:	
£	
11,700 × 18% (W)	2,106.00
87,400 × 28%	24,472.00
99,100	
Capital gains tax payable	26,578.00

Remaining basic rate band

	£
Basic rate band	32,010
Plus: Gift Aid donation (£400 × 100/80)	500
Extended basic rate band	32,510
Less: Taxable income	(20,810)
Remaining basic rate band	11,700

Tutorial note

The taxable income falls below the basic rate band threshold, therefore there is some of the basic rate band remaining to match against the taxable gains.

However, be careful as the basic rate band will be extended by the gross Gift Aid donation.

Taxable gains fall partly into the remaining basic rate band and partly into the higher rate band. The capital gains tax liability is therefore calculated in two parts at 18% and 28%.

108 KIESWETTER

(a) The statement is true.

Tutorial note

For the purposes of the AAT assessment, all animals including greyhounds, racehorses etc, are wasting chattels, so they are exempt assets.

(b) The statement is false.

Tutorial note

Cars are exempt assets.

(c) The answer is B

Working

	£
Capital gains for the year	20,000
Less: Capital losses for the year	(5,200)
Less: Capital losses brought forward (restricted)	(3,900)
Net gains	10,900
Less: Annual exempt amount	(10,900)
Taxable gains	Nil

Capital losses carried forward are £3,100 (£7,000 b/f – £3,900 used)

Tutorial note

All current year losses must be set against current year capital gains, even if they waste the annual exempt amount.

However, when capital losses are brought forward, their use can be restricted to allow the taxpayer to use up all of their annual exempt amount

109 JOANNA

	True	False
Capital gains are taxed at 18% for all taxpayers.		✓
If a taxpayer does not use their annual exempt amount in 2012/13 they can bring it forward to use in 2013/14.		✓
Brought forward capital losses are restricted to allow full use of the annual exempt amount for the year.	✓	

Tutorial note

The rate of capital gains tax depends on the level of the taxable income.

Taxable gains are taxed after taxable income.

Taxable gains falling into the basic rate band are taxed at 18%. Those gains falling into the higher rate band are taxed at 28%.

If a taxpayer does not use his annual exempt amount for capital gains tax purposes, it cannot be carried forward or backwards and it cannot be given away. It is wasted (i.e. lost).

110 ALICE

	£
Proceeds	52,000
Less: Selling costs – auctioneers fees (£52,000 × 2%)	(1,040)
	50,960
Less: Cost	(35,700)
Purchase costs – legal fees	(250)
Chargeable gain	15,010
Less: Annual exempt amount	(10,900)
Taxable gain	4,110
Capital gains tax (£4,110 × 28%)	1,150.80

Tutorial note

Accountant's fees for agreeing a capital gains tax computation are not a valid cost for capital gain purposes.

Capital gains tax is calculated at 28% as Alice is a higher rate taxpayer.

111 KEVIN

The answer is C.

Tutorial note

Only the annual exempt amount can be deducted from capital gains, not the personal allowance.

Brought forward capital losses are restricted to protect the annual exempt amount, not current year losses.

112 RASHIDA

	Capital loss b/f £	*Capital gain 2013/14* £	*Capital loss 2013/14* £	*Capital loss c/f* £
1	7,560	25,000	12,290	5,750
2	Nil	16,500	21,000	4,500
3	12,900	14,780	8,000	12,900
4	5,200	13,700	Nil	2,400

Workings

		£
(W1)	Capital gains for the year	25,000
	Less: Capital losses for the year	(12,290)
	Less: Capital losses brought forward (restricted)	(1,810)
	Net gains	10,900
	Less: Annual exempt amount	(10,900)
	Taxable gains	Nil

Capital losses carried forward are £5,750 (£7,560 b/f – £1,810 used)

		£
(W2)	Capital gains for the year	16,500
	Less: Capital losses for the year	(21,000)
	Net loss c/f	(4,500)

		£
(W3)	Capital gains for the year	14,780
	Less: Capital losses for the year	(8,000)
	Less: Capital losses brought forward	Nil
	Net gains	6,780
	Less: Annual exempt amount (restricted)	(6,780)
	Taxable gains	Nil

Capital losses carried forward are £12,900

		£
(W4)	Capital gains for the year	13,700
	Less: Capital losses for the year	Nil
	Less: Capital losses brought forward (restricted)	(2,800)
	Net gains	10,900
	Less: Annual exempt amount	(10,900)
	Taxable gains	Nil

Capital losses carried forward are £2,400 (£5,200 b/f – £2,800 used)

Tutorial note

All current year losses must be set against current year capital gains, even if they waste the annual exempt amount.

However, when capital losses are brought forward, their use can be restricted to allow the taxpayer to use up their entire annual exempt amount

113 ARLENE

	£
Gains	31,500
Capital losses	(4,500)
	27,000
Less: Annual exempt amount	(10,900)
Taxable gains	16,100

	£		
	7,200	× 18%	1,296
(£16,100 – £7,200)	8,900	× 28%	2,492
	16,100		3,788

Due date of payment	31.1.2015

114 HUEY, DUEY AND LOUIE

Taxpayer	Gain 2013/14	Loss 2012/13 b/f	Relieve all loss	Relieve some loss	Relieve no loss
Huey	£21,450	£6,550	✓		
Duey	£10,230	£5,150			✓
Louie	£14,790	£7,820		✓	

Tutorial note

Capital losses brought forward only have to be used to reduce the net gains for the year down to the level of the annual exempt amount.

115 TINEKE

Occupation	Non-occupation
31.5.2005 – 31.12.2005	1.12.08 – 31.12.2010
1.1.2006 – 31.12.2007 (working abroad)	
1.1.2008 – 31.8.2008 (working away in UK)	
1.9.2008 – 30.11.2008	
1.1.2011 – 31.12.2013 (Last 36 months)	

Tutorial note

A taxpayer's principal private residence is exempt for the periods when it is occupied or deemed occupied.

The last 36 months of ownership are always deemed occupation even if the taxpayer has another residence by then.

Other deemed residence periods:

(i) Any period working abroad – this covers Tineke's two years abroad.

(ii) Up to a total of 4 years working elsewhere in the UK – this covers Tineke's eight months working away in the UK.

(iii) Up to a total of 3 years for any reason.

These periods must be preceded at some time by actual occupation and followed by actual occupation (except occupation after the absence is not insisted on for (i) and (ii) if the taxpayer cannot return to their residence due to being moved elsewhere to work).

This means that the 3 years for any reason cannot be applied to the time Tineke lives with her boyfriend as she does not return to the flat.

116 RENATA

Occupation	Non-occupation
1.5.2003 – 31.12.2006	1.1.2007 – 30.6.2010
1.7.2010 – 1.7.2013 (Last 36 months)	

Tutorial note

A taxpayer's principal private residence is exempt for the periods when it is occupied or deemed occupied.

The last 36 months of ownership are always deemed occupation even if the taxpayer has another residence by then.

This is the only period of deemed occupation allowed as Renata does not work abroad, nor elsewhere in the UK and the 3 years for any reason cannot be applied to the time Renata lives with her sister as she does not return to the flat.

117 YASMIN

	All treated as occupation	Part treated as occupation	Not treated as occupation
(a) Yasmin spent 10 years working abroad.	✓		
(b) George spent 4 years motorcycling around the world.		✓	
(c) The last 4 years of Owen's ownership in which he did not live in the house.		✓	
(d) Ian spent 5 years working elsewhere in the UK	✓		
(e) Irina moved out of her house and spent 2 years living in her boyfriend's house. After they split up she moved back to live with her parents and never moved back to her own house which she sold 5 years later.			
– for the 2 years living with boyfriend			✓
– for the 5 years living with parents		✓	

Tutorial note

The last 36 months of ownership are always deemed occupation even if the taxpayer has another residence by then.

Other deemed residence periods:

(i) Any period working abroad

(ii) Up to a total of 4 years working elsewhere in the UK.

(iii) Up to a total of 3 years for any reason.

These periods must be preceded at some time by actual occupation and followed by actual occupation (except occupation after the absence is not insisted on for (i) and (ii) if the taxpayer cannot return to their residence due to being moved elsewhere to work.)

Yasmin is covered by (i).

George is not covered by (i) as he is not working, however he can claim (iii) and exempt some of the period of absence.

Owen's last 4 years is partly covered by the last 36 months rule.

Ian is covered by (ii) and the last year by (iii).

Irina's 2 years living with her boyfriend are not covered as she does not actually reoccupy the property at any time after the period of absence.

Irina's 5 years living with parents is partly covered by the last 36 months rule.

118 ESME

(a)	The total period of ownership of the house is (in months)	120
(b)	The period of actual and deemed residence is (in months)	96
(c)	The chargeable gain on the sale of the house is (to the nearest £)	£49,000

Workings

(W1) **Total ownership**

The house is owned from 1 July 2003 to 1 July 2013 = 10 years or 120 months

(W2) **Periods of residence and deemed residence**

Residence and deemed residence	*Mths*	*Non-occupation*	*Mths*
1.7.2003 – 30.6.2005	24	1.7.2008 – 30.6.2010	24
1.7.2005 – 30.6.2006 (Part of 3 years any reason)	12		
1.7. 2006 – 30.6.2008	24		
1.7.2010 – 1.7.2013 (Last 36 months)	36		
Total	96		

(W3) **Capital gain on sale of house**

	£
Proceeds	285,000
Less: Cost	(40,000)
	245,000
Less: PPR exemption 96/120 × £245,000	(196,000)
Chargeable gain	49,000

Tutorial note

The last 36 months of ownership are always deemed occupation even if the taxpayer has another residence by then.

Other deemed residence periods:

(i) Any period working abroad

(ii) Up to a total of 4 years working elsewhere in the UK.

(iii) Up to a total of 3 years for any reason.

These periods must be preceded at some time by actual occupation and followed by actual occupation (except occupation after the absence is not insisted on for (i) and (ii) if the taxpayer cannot return to their residence due to being moved elsewhere to work.)

Esme cannot claim the "working abroad" period as deemed occupation as she was not working. However, she is always entitled to the last 36 months and the period abroad can be covered by 3 years for any reason rule.

The remainder of the 3 years for any reason cannot be used to cover the period while living with her boyfriend as she does not actually reoccupy the property at any time after the period of absence.

119 LYNNETTE

Lynnette is away from her house for 12 years and never returns.

As she cannot return to her house because of her job, she can claim deemed occupation for 4 years working elsewhere in the UK. However, she cannot have the 3 years for any reason as she does not return to the house.

The last 3 years of ownership are always deemed occupation.

Total occupation plus deemed occupation is 15 years out of the 20 owned.

	£
Capital gain	360,000
Less: Principal Private Residence exemption (15/20)	(270,000)
Chargeable gain	90,000

Section 3

AQ2013: MOCK ASSESSMENT QUESTIONS

TASK 1 **(9 MARKS)**

Oliver Reeves was unemployed until 6 June 2013, when he started a new job as a salesman with an annual salary of £27,000.

As part of his remuneration package, he was provided with the following benefits:

- From 6 November 2013, a Ford car. The list price of the car is £15,500 and Oliver paid his company £100 per month in respect of his private use of the car.
- The CO_2 emissions are 153 g/km and it has a diesel engine.
- The company pays for all the running costs of the car including the fuel. Oliver paid his company £30 per month towards the provision of diesel.
- From 6 December 2013, a second car for his wife. The list price of the car is £12,000; however the company bought it second hand for £9,000. The CO_2 emissions are 93 g/km.
- It has a petrol engine; but the company does not pay for any private fuel on this car.

(i)	What is the scale percentage for Oliver's Ford car?	%
(ii)	What is the taxable benefit for the use of the Ford car?	£
(iii)	What is the taxable benefit for the fuel provided by the company?	£
(iv)	What is the scale charge percentage for Oliver's wife's car?	%
(v)	What price is used to calculate the car benefit on Oliver's wife's car?	£
(vi)	What is the taxable benefit for Oliver's wife's car?	£

TASK 2 **(10 MARKS)**

(a) What is the taxable benefit for each of the employment benefits received by the employees listed below?

(i)	Carol, a basic rate taxpayer, receives £55 per week in childcare vouchers from her employer. The vouchers are for a registered child care provider.	£
(ii)	Bill received £1,800 as a loan from his employer in 2013/14. He pays interest on the loan at the rate of 2%.	£
(iii)	Les borrowed a digital camera from his employer on 6 June 2013 until 5 April 2014 to use on his holidays and for family occasions. The market value of the camera on 6 June 2013 was £1,200.	£
(iv)	From 6 January 2014, Sarah was provided with a company loan of £20,000 on which she pays interest at 2.5% per annum.	£
(v)	Majid was provided with accommodation by his employer. The house has an annual value £4,200 and the employer pays a rent of £250 per month. Her employer also paid a utility bill for the house of £180 during 2013/14. Majid moved out when he left his employment on 5 December 2013.	£

(b) Rose has asked you to advise her which of the following benefits, provided to employees earning over £12,000 per year, are exempt.

Tick one box on each line.

	Exempt	Not exempt
Use of a company car with CO_2 emissions of 72 g/km		
A place in the company's workplace based nursery for two children		
One mobile telephone for each employee and each spouse		
Provision of bicycle helmets for staff earning below £20,000 p.a.		
Staff Christmas party costing £75 per employee		
Relocation expenses of £7,500		

(c) For each statement, tick either employment or self employment.

	Employment	Self employment
Being provided with paid holidays		
Having to correct poor work at your own expense		
Providing your own tools and equipment		

TASK 3 **(10 MARKS)**

(a) Which of the following statements are true and which false?

Tick the correct box for each statement.

	True	False
The amount of rent you can receive which is tax free under the rent-a-room scheme is £4,500.		
The rent-a-room limit is compared to the gross rents before deduction of expenses.		
A husband and wife jointly owning a property cannot have a rent-a-room limit each to match against a lodger's rental income. However, if two friends purchase a house together and rent to a lodger, they can have a rent-a-room limit each.		
Wear and tear allowance is calculated as: 10% (Rents received – Water rates and council tax paid by the landlord)		

(b) Steven Mason has three properties, details of which are as follows:

Four bedroom house:

1 This furnished house is rented out for £780 per month. The property was occupied throughout 2013/14. Steven paid council tax of £800 and water rates of £300 for 2013/14.

2 The only other expense paid by Steven in respect of the house was 7% commission to the agent on the rent received.

One bedroom flat:

3 This unfurnished flat is rented out for £415 per month. The property was occupied until 5 November 2013 when the tenants moved out without paying the last month's rent. It is highly unlikely that Steven will be able to recover this debt. New tenants moved in on 6 January 2014 when the rent had increased to £435 per month.

4 Steven paid a cleaner £60 per month to clean this property throughout 2013/14.

Two bedroom house:

5 This house was rented out from 6 July 2013 for £610 per month. Steven purchased furniture for £5,000 to go in the house.

6 Steven paid council tax of £700 and £225 water rates in respect of the house for 2013/14. He also paid interest of £280.

Calculate the profit or loss made on each property using the following table.

Do not use brackets or minus signs and if you feel any items are not allowable please insert a zero "0".

	Four bedroom house £	*One bedroom flat* £	*Two bedroom house* £
Income			
Expenses:			
Commission			
Council tax			
Water rates			
Cleaning			
Furniture			
Interest			
Wear and tear allowance			
PROFIT or LOSS			

TASK 4 **(6 MARKS)**

(a) Place the following types of investment income in the correct column in the table below.

- Premium Bond prize
- Interest from 3½% War loan (a government stock)
- Bank interest received
- Interest from an ISA
- Interest from an NS&I bank account

Received net	**Received gross**	**Exempt**

(b) During 2013/14, Lexie received interest of £240 from her building society account and £370 from her NS&I bank account

The tax deducted from this interest totals:

A £48.00

B £60.00

C £122.00

D £152.50

(c) In 2013/14, Joe received £13,500 dividends from his investments in UK companies.

He has other taxable income of £142,000.

What is the tax liability arising on his dividend income?

(d) Jason received NS&I interest of £150 and won £20,000 on a National Lottery scratch card in 2013/14.

How much of this income should he enter into his income tax computation?

A £150 for NS&I and £20,000 for the winnings

B £187 for NS&I and £Nil for the winnings

C £150 for NS&I and £Nil for the winnings

D £187 for NS&I and £20,000 for the winnings

TASK 5 **(12 MARKS)**

Joseph was born on 1 September 1961.

(1) In 2013/14 he received a salary of £91,000 until 31 December 2013 when he received a pay rise of 4%.

(2) He received a bonus payment on 31 March 2013 of £18,000 relating to his employer's year ended 31 December 2012 and another payment on 31 March 2014 for £22,400 relating to his employer's year ended 31 December 2013.

(3) There was no occupational pension scheme available with his employer so Joseph paid £720 into a private pension each month. His employer paid £350 per month into the scheme.

(4) He also contributed £100 a month to charity via the company's payroll giving scheme.

(5) He pays £1,020 per annum in subscriptions of which £580 is paid to the Chartered Institute of Information Technology and £440 to his local golf club where he often meets clients for lunch and a round of golf.

(5) He makes a donation to charity under the Gift aid scheme of £500 per year.

(6) He receives building society interest of £1,080 and interest of £400 from an ISA account.

(7) He has sold shares during the year making a gain of £5,000

Complete the following table to calculate Joseph's taxable income for 2013/14. You should use whole pounds only. If your answer is zero please include '0'. Do not use brackets or minus signs.

	£
Salary	
Bonus	
Contribution to personal pension scheme	
Employer's pension contribution	
Payroll giving scheme	
Subscription to Chartered Institute of Information Technology	
Subscription to Golf Club	
Gift Aid donation	
Building society interest	
ISA interest	
Gain on shares	
Personal allowance	
Taxable income	

TASK 6 **(10 MARKS)**

Rita, aged 36, is employed as a receptionist with a gross annual salary of £36,980. On 21 April 2013 she received a bonus of £4,220 which related to her performance during the year ended 31 March 2013. She has paid £6,700 of PAYE during the year.

Rita received dividends of £2,025 and ISA interest of £6,980

Enter your answer and workings into the table below to calculate Rita's income tax payable for 2013/14.

TASK 7 **(10 MARKS)**

(a) Katie has written to you with the following query:

> 'Please can you explain to me how my tax payments are calculated as I do not understand what needs paying and when?
>
> My income tax liability was £8,900 for 2012/13. According to your latest calculation my income tax liability will be £10,200 for 2013/14. In addition I have to pay capital gains tax of £3,350 in respect of capital disposals made in 2013/14.
>
> Could you please let me know what I should pay and the due dates for payment?
>
> Many thanks
>
> Katie

You need to respond appropriately to her query.

(b) Joachim asks whether the following statements are true or false.

Tick the correct box for each statement.

	True	False
An individual who does not receive a tax return must inform HMRC of any untaxed income received in 2013/14 by 31 December 2014.		
Payments on account are compulsory in 2013/14 for all taxpayers whose tax payable in 2012/13 exceeded £1,000.		

(c) Which ONE of the following statements is not correct?

A The AAT expects its members to maintain an objective outlook

B You must follow the rules of confidentiality even after a client relationship has ended

C An AAT member has a professional duty only to their client and not society as a whole

D An AAT member advising on tax issues has a duty to both their client and to HMRC

(d) If an AAT member suspects his client of money laundering which one of the following actions must he take?

A He should discuss his suspicions with the client

B He should report his suspicions to his employer's Money Laundering Reporting Officer

C He should report his suspicions to HMRC

D He should report his suspicions to the AAT

TASK 8 **(7 MARKS)**

Complete the tax return below as far as the following information permits.

Trevor Oldham was employed from 1 June 2013 as a salesman by Target plc. His gross annual salary was £28,000 and he received commission of £2,500 in 2013/14. PAYE of £3,705 was deducted from his salary.

He was provided with a company car from 1 July 2013 with an annual benefit value of £5,625.

He was also provided with private medical insurance which cost his employer £300 in 2013/14. Trevor paid a £190 subscription to his trade association.

Employment

Tax year 6 April 2013 to 5 April 2014

Your name

Your Unique Taxpayer Reference (UTR)

Complete an *Employment* page for each employment or directorship

1 Pay from this employment – the total from your P45 or P60 – *before tax was taken off*

£ . 0 0

2 UK tax taken off pay in box 1

£ . 0 0

3 Tips and other payments not on your P60 – *read the Employment notes*

£ . 0 0

4 PAYE tax reference of your employer (on your P45/P60)

/

5 Your employer's name

6 If you were a company director, put 'X' in the box

7 And, if the company was a close company, put 'X' in the box

8 If you are a part-time teacher in England or Wales and are on the Repayment of Teachers' Loans Scheme for this employment, put 'X' in the box

Benefits from your employment – use your form P11D (or equivalent information)

9 Company cars and vans – *the total 'cash equivalent' amount*

£ . 0 0

10 Fuel for company cars and vans – *the total 'cash equivalent' amount*

£ . 0 0

11 Private medical and dental insurance – *the total 'cash equivalent' amount*

£ . 0 0

12 Vouchers, credit cards and excess mileage allowance

£ . 0 0

13 Goods and other assets provided by your employer – *the total value or amount*

£ . 0 0

14 Accommodation provided by your employer – *the total value or amount*

£ . 0 0

15 Other benefits (including interest-free and low interest loans) – *the total 'cash equivalent' amount*

£ . 0 0

16 Expenses payments received and balancing charges

£ . 0 0

Employment expenses

17 Business travel and subsistence expenses

£ . 0 0

18 Fixed deductions for expenses

£ . 0 0

19 Professional fees and subscriptions

£ . 0 0

20 Other expenses and capital allowances

£ . 0 0

Shares schemes, employment lump sums, compensation, deductions and Seafarers' Earnings Deduction are on the *Additional information* pages enclosed in the tax return pack.

SA102 2013 Page E 1 HMRC 12/12

TASK 9 **(12 MARKS)**

(a) Paul inherited seven acres of land in August 2010 from his grandfather.

The land had cost his grandfather £15,000 but was worth £49,000 (the probate value) when Paul received it.

Paul sold three acres in November 2013 for £75,000 when the remaining four acres were worth £125,000. He paid auctioneer's commission of 8% when he sold the asset.

What is the gain on this asset?

A £51,572

B £48,000

C £50,625

D £63,375

(b) Artem bought a holiday home in March 2009 for £174,000 plus stamp duty of £1,740.

She spent £20,000 on extending the property in April 2011. She has paid insurance premiums totalling £3,750 during the time she has owned the asset.

She sold the property at auction for £355,000 in March 2014 incurring selling costs of £6,500. Artem was disappointed with this price as the property had been valued at £400,000 before the auction.

What is the gain on this asset?

A £149,010

B £197,760

C £154,500

D £152,760

(c) True or false:

Accountancy fees for calculating capital gains tax are an allowable selling expense when disposing of an asset.

(d) Rose disposed of the following assets in 2013/14.

For each asset, calculate the gain before annual exempt amount or the allowable loss:

(i)	Sold a racehorse for £25,000. She had originally purchased the racehorse for £8,900.	£
(ii)	Sold an antique table to her neighbour for £5,000. She paid £50 commission on the sale. She originally purchased the table for £11,000. The table got scratched while she owned it (hence the low proceeds).	£
(iii)	Sold a holiday cottage in Devon for £110,000. She originally purchased the cottage for £50,000 and extended it two years later which cost £8,000.	£

TASK 10 **(8 MARKS)**

Paul disposed of 9,000 shares in Sun Ltd for £5 per share in October 2013.

He acquired the shares as follows:

		Number of shares	*Cost*
October 2009	Purchase	1,000	£1,250
January 2010	Purchase	3,000	£6,300
December 2011	Bonus issue	1 for 3	
January 2012	Purchase	5,000	£15,200

In June 2011, Sun Ltd had a rights issue of 1 for 5 shares for £2.25 per share. Paul did not take up the rights shares.

Clearly showing the balance of shares, and their value, to carry forward calculate the gain or loss made on these shares.

All workings must be shown in your calculations.

TASK 11 **(6 MARKS)**

(a) Harold bought a house for £101,000 on 1 March 1992.

He lived in the house with his wife until 31 March 1996 when they went to work in Newcastle.

He returned to the house on 1 April 2005 and lived in it until 31 October 2011 when he moved in with his elderly parents.

The house was sold for £336,000 on 1 May 2013.

What is the taxable gain assuming Harold has no other disposals in 2013/14?

A £11,305

B £235,000

C £44,612

D £22,205

E £212,795

(b) Margaret has disposed of several capital assets in 2013/14 and realised the following gains and losses:

	Disposal to:	£
Chargeable gain	Aunt	23,000
Chargeable gain	Unconnected person	14,500
Allowable loss	Brother	(3,000)
Allowable loss	Friend	(2,600)

Margaret has unutilised capital losses relating to 2012/13 of £5,600.

(i)	What are Margaret's taxable gains for 2013/14?	£
(ii)	What is the capital loss remaining to carry forward to 2014/15?	£

(c) Currie has taxable income of £30,000 for 2013/14. He has made gains of £26,000.

(i)	What is Currie's capital gains tax liability for 2013/14?	£
(ii)	What is the due date of payment?	

Section 4

AQ2013: MOCK ASSESSMENT ANSWERS

TASK 1

	Question	Answer	Working
(i)	What is the scale percentage for Oliver's Ford car?	% 25	W1
(ii)	What is the taxable benefit for the use of the Ford car?	£1,115	W2
(iii)	What is the taxable benefit for the fuel provided by the company?	£2,198	W3
(iv)	What is the scale charge percentage for Oliver's wife's car?	% 10	W4
(v)	What price is used to calculate the car benefit on Oliver's wife's car?	£12,000	W5
(vi)	What is the taxable benefit for Oliver's wife's car?	£400	W6

Workings

(W1) **Ford scale percentage**

CO_2 emissions are rounded down to 150 g/km.

Appropriate percentage = (14% diesel + (150 – 95) × 1/5) = 25%

(W2) **Ford taxable benefit**

Car has been available for 5 months of the tax year.

	£
£15,500 × 25% × 5/12	1,615
Less: Contribution in respect of private use (£100 × 5 months)	(500)
Car benefit	1,115

Tutorial note

The car has CO_2 emissions in excess of 94 g/km.

The appropriate percentage is therefore calculated in the normal way (i.e. a scale percentage of 11% for petrol cars and 14% for diesel cars, plus 1% for each complete 5 g/km above 95 g/km up to a maximum percentage of 35%).

As the car has not been available all year, the benefit must be time apportioned.

Contributions in respect of the private use of the car are an allowable deduction from the benefit.

(W3) **Ford fuel benefit**

Fuel benefit = (£21,100 × 25% × 5/12) = £2,198

Tutorial note

The appropriate percentage for the fuel benefit is the same as that calculated for the car benefit. This is applied to a fixed scale figure of £21,100.

As the car has not been available all year, the benefit must be time apportioned.

A contribution towards the provision of private petrol is not an allowable deduction from the benefit.

(W4) **Oliver's wife's car scale percentage**

Appropriate percentage = 10%.

Tutorial note

The car has CO_2 emissions of between 76 and 94 g/km and is therefore a low emission car.

The appropriate percentage for a petrol car is 10%, and 13% for a diesel car.

(W5) **Oliver's wife's car price**

Price used to calculate the car benefit = £12,000.

Tutorial note

The second hand price actually paid by the company is not relevant. The car benefit is based on the original manufacturer's list price.

(W6) **Oliver's wife's car – taxable benefit**

Car has been available for 4 months of the tax year.

	£
£12,000 × 10% × 4/12	400

Tutorial note

This benefit is taxable on Oliver.

TASK 2

(a) What is the taxable benefit for each of the employment benefits received by the employees listed below?

(i)	Carol, a basic rate taxpayer, receives £55 per week in childcare vouchers from her employer. The vouchers are for a registered child care provider.	£Nil	W1
(ii)	Bill received £1,800 as a loan from his employer in 2013/14. He pays interest on the loan at the rate of 2%.	£Nil	W2
(iii)	Les borrowed a digital camera from his employer on 6 June 2013 until 5 April 2014 to use on his holidays and for family occasions. The market value of the camera on 6 June 2013 was £1,200.	£200	W3
(iv)	From 6 January 2014, Sarah was provided with a company loan of £20,000 on which she pays interest at 2.5% per annum.	£75	W4
(v)	Majid was provided with accommodation by his employer. The house has an annual value £4,200 and the employer pays a rent of £250 per month. Her employer also paid a utility bill for the house of £180 during 2013/14. Majid moved out when he left his employment on 5 December 2013.	£2,980	W5

Workings

(W1) **Childcare vouchers**

Taxable benefit = £Nil

Tutorial note

Childcare vouchers up to £55 per week spent with an approved child minder are an exempt benefit for a basic rate taxpayer.

(W2) **Company loan**

Taxable benefit = £Nil

Tutorial note

Loans which do not exceed £5,000 at any time in the tax year are an exempt benefit.

(W3) **Use of camera**

Taxable benefit = (£1,200 × 20% × 10/12) = £200

Tutorial note

The benefit for the use of a company asset such as a camera is 20% of the market value of the asset when first made available to the employee.

As the camera was only made available to Les from 6 June 2013, the benefit is time apportioned.

(W4) **Company loan**

Taxable benefit = (£20,000 × (4% – 2.5%) × 3/12) = £75

Tutorial note

Beneficial loan interest benefit is calculated as follows:

= Outstanding loan × the difference between the official rate of interest (4% in 2013/14) and the actual interest rate paid by the employee.

However, as the loan was provided nine months into the tax year 2013/14, the benefit must be time apportioned as the rates of interest quoted are annual rates of interest.

(W5) **Accommodation benefit**

	£
Higher of:	
(i) Annual value = £4,200	
(ii) Rent paid by employer = (£250 × 12) = £3,000	
Only available for 8 months of the year:	
Basic charge benefit = (£4,200 × 8/12)	2,800
Utility bill paid for by employer – benefit = cost to employer	180
Total accommodation benefit	2,980

(b) Rose has asked you to advise her which of the following benefits, provided to employees earning over £12,000 per year, are exempt.

Tick one box on each line.

	Exempt	Not exempt
Use of a company car with CO_2 emissions of 72 g/km		✓
A place in the company's workplace based nursery for two children	✓	
One mobile telephone for each employee and each spouse		✓
Provision of bicycle helmets for staff earning below £20,000 p.a.		✓
Staff Christmas party costing £75 per employee	✓	
Relocation expenses of £7,500	✓	

Tutorial note

A car with CO_2 emissions of less than 75 g/km is a "very low emission car". The provision of such a car is not however an exempt benefit. The appropriate % will be 5% for a petrol car and 8% for a diesel car.

A place in the workplace nursery is an exempt benefit, regardless of the number of children or cost of provision. The limits that apply depending on the rate at which the employee pays tax relate to childcare vouchers and childcare with approved carers other than in the workplace nursery.

Only one mobile phone per employee is treated as an exempt benefit.

The provision of cycle helmets is an exempt benefit provided they are available to all staff generally. It will not be exempt if it is conditional on the amount earned.

Staff entertaining of up to £150 per head per tax year is an exempt benefit.

Relocation expenses of up to £8,000 are an exempt benefit.

(c) For each statement, tick either employment or self employment.

	Employment	**Self employment**
Being provided with paid holidays	✓	
Having to correct poor work at your own expense		✓
Providing your own tools and equipment		✓

Key answer tips

You need to make sure that you know the factors that HMRC will consider to decide the status of an individual with regard to employment or self employment

TASK 3

(a) Which of the following statements are true and which false?

Tick the correct box for each statement.

	True	False
The amount of rent you can receive which is tax free under the rent-a-room scheme is £4,500.		✓
The rent-a-room limit is compared to the gross rents before deduction of expenses.	✓	
A husband and wife jointly owning a property cannot have a rent-a-room limit each to match against a lodger's rental income. However, if two friends purchase a house together and rent to a lodger, they can have a rent-a-room limit each.		✓
Wear and tear allowance is calculated as: 10% (Rents received – Water rates and council tax paid by the landlord)	✓	

Tutorial note

The tax free limit for rent-a-room relief is £4,250 for 2013/14, not £4,500.

Only one rent-a-room relief limit is available per residential property lived in as a home.

It is not therefore possible to have two rent-a-room limits for a house, regardless of whether or not the owners of the property are married.

(b)

	Four bedroom house £	*One bedroom flat* £	*Two bedroom house* £
Income	9,360	3,795	5,490
Expenses:			
Commission	655	0	0
Council tax	800	0	700
Water rates	300	0	225
Cleaning	0	720	0
Furniture	0	0	0
Interest	0	0	280
Wear and tear allowance	826	0	457
PROFIT or LOSS	6,779	3,075	3828

Workings

	Four bedroom house £	*One bedroom flat* £	*Two bedroom house* £
Income:			
(£780 × 12 months)	9,360		
(£415 × 7 months)		2,905	
(£435 × 3 months)		1,305	
Less: Bad debt (Note)		(415)	
		3,795	
(£610 × 9 months)			5,490
Expenses:			
Council tax	(800)		(700)
Water rates	(300)		(225)
Agents commission (7% × £9,360)	(655)		
Cleaning		(720)	
Interest			(280)
Wear and tear allowance			
(£9,360 – £800 – £300) × 10%	(826)		
(£5,490 – £700 – £225) × 10%			(457)
Rental profit	6,779	3,075	3,828

Tutorial note

Rental income is assessed on an accruals basis; therefore all of the rent accrued should be brought into the computation.

However, there is relief for the rent which is irrecoverable. It can be deducted as a bad debt.

Note that if in the CBT there is a proforma already set up with narrative, and there is no bad debt line, it is acceptable to just include in the rental income section the net rents actually received rather than two entries of rents accrued and the bad debt deduction.

A wear and tear allowance is given for furnished properties.

The allowance available is:

10% × (Rent received – Water rates and council tax paid by the landlord)

TASK 4

(a) **Sources of income**

Received net	Received gross	Exempt
Bank interest received	Interest from 3½% war loan Interest from an NS&I bank account	Premium Bond prize Interest from an ISA

(b) The answer is B

Tutorial note

NS&I interest is received gross.

The building society interest is received net of 20% tax.

Hence the tax deducted = (£240 × 20/80) = £60.00

(c) **Income tax on dividend income**

	£
Dividend income:	
From UK companies (£13,500 × 100/90)	15,000
Income tax on dividend income only: (Note)	
(£150,000 – £142,000) = £8,000 × 32.5%	2,600.00
(£157,000 – £150,000) = £7,000 × 37.5%	2,625.00
Income tax liability on dividend income	5,225.00

Tutorial note

As his taxable income including the dividends exceeds £150,000, Joe is an additional rate taxpayer.

Dividends that fall into the higher rate band will be taxed at 32.5%. Dividends that fall above £150,000 will be taxed at 37.5%.

(d) The answer is C.

Tutorial note

NS&I interest is received gross and scratch card winnings are exempt from income tax.

TASK 5

	£
Salary	91,910
Bonus	22,400
Contribution to personal pension scheme	0
Employer's pension contribution	0
Payroll giving scheme	1,200
Subscription to Chartered Institute of Information Technology	580
Subscription to Golf Club	0
Gift Aid donation	0
Building society interest	1,350
ISA interest	0
Gain on shares	0
Personal allowance	8,213
Taxable income	105,667

Workings

(W1) **Taxable income**

	£
Salary (£91,000 × 9/12) + (£91,000 × 1.04 × 3/12)	91,910
Bonus (Received 31 March 2014)	22,400
Personal pension scheme (not an allowable deduction)	0
Payroll giving scheme (12 × £100)	(1,200)
Professional subscription only	(580)
BSI (£1,080 × 100/80)	1,350
ISA interest (exempt)	0
Gain (not part of taxable income)	0
Total income	113,880
Personal allowance (W2)	(8,213)
Taxable income	105,667

(W2) **Personal allowance**

	£	£
Personal allowance		9,440
Net income (= Total income)	113,880	
Less: Gross personal pension contribution		
(£720 × 12 × 100/80)	(10,800)	
Gross Gift aid (£500 × 100/80)	(625)	
Adjusted net income	102,455	
Less: Limit	(100,000)	
Excess	2,455 × 50%	(1,227)
Adjusted PA		8,213

Tutorial note

The tax year runs from 6 April 2013 to 5 April 2014 and Joseph's salary changes after nine months of this period. The salary must therefore be time apportioned.

The bonus is assessed in the tax year of receipt.

Unlike contributions into an occupational pension scheme, contributions into a personal pension scheme are not an allowable deduction from employment income.

Instead, relief for basic rate tax is given at source and higher rate (and additional rate relief, if applicable) is given by extending the basic rate and higher rate band thresholds by the gross personal pension contribution. The gross personal pension contribution is also a deduction from net income when calculating the personal allowance.

Employers' contributions to pension schemes are an exempt benefit

The contribution to charity under the payroll giving scheme is an allowable deduction from employment income.

However, donations under the Gift Aid scheme are not relieved against employment income. Relief is given in the same way as for personal pension contributions by extending the basic rate and higher rate thresholds and by reducing the net income when calculating the personal allowance.

The donation to the Chartered Institute of Information Technology will be an allowable deduction for employment income purposes. However, the golf membership will not be allowable for tax, despite there being a work related purpose for visiting the golf club.

TASK 6

Rita – Income tax computation – 2013/14

	Total	*Other*	*Dividends*
	£	£	£
Salary	36,980		
Bonus (received 21 April 2013)	4,220		
Employment income	41,200	41,200	
Dividends (£2,025 × 100/90)	2,250		2,250
ISA interest – exempt	Nil		
Net income	43,450	41,200	2,250
Less: PA	(9,440)	(9,440)	
Taxable income	34,010	31,760	2,250

Income tax:		
Other income	31,760 at 20%	6,352.00
Savings	250 at 10%	25.00
	32,010	
Savings	2,000 at 32.5%	650.00
	34,010	
Income tax liability		7,027.00
Less : Tax deducted at source		
Dividend tax credit (£2,250 × 10%)		(225.00)
PAYE		(6,700.00)
Income tax payable		102.00

Key answer tips

It is important when using this type of layout to analyse the taxable income into "other income", "savings" and "dividends" as different rates of tax apply to the different sources of income.

Note that:

- the above layout should be possible if the CBT gives five columns to complete the calculation
- the total lines do not have to be inserted in the real CBT
- you may find it useful to do the computation on paper first before inputting on screen

TASK 7

(a) Dear Katie,

Payments on account of the tax liability for any year are paid by 31 January in that tax year, and by 31 July following the tax year. This is based on an estimate, using the preceding tax years' payable.

Therefore, when you made your tax payments on 31 January 2013 and 31 July 2013 for 2012/13, this was based on your liability for 2011/12.

When the final figures are sent to HMRC, if these two instalments are not enough to cover the full liability, a balancing payment is due on 31 January following the tax year.

For 2013/14 your payments due will therefore be:

31 January 2014	(£8,900 × 1/2)	£4,450
31 July 2014	(£8,900 × 1/2)	£4,450
31 January 2015	(£10,200 – £8,900)	£1,300

In addition, on 31 January 2015, all of the capital gains tax liability of £3,350 is due for payment as capital gains tax is never paid in instalments.

Finally on 31 January 2015 you will have to make the first payment on account of your 2014/15 liability. This will be £5,100 as it is based on half of your 2013/14 liability of £10,200.

The total amount due on 31 January 2015 will be £9,750 (£1,300 + £3,350 + £5,100).

I hope this makes things clearer. If you have any queries please do not hesitate to contact me.

Best regards

AAT Student

(b) Joachim asks whether the following statements are true or false.

Tick the correct box for each statement.

	True	False
An individual who does not receive a tax return must inform HMRC of any untaxed income received in 2012/13 by 31 December 2014.		✓
Payments on account are compulsory in 2013/14 for all taxpayers whose tax payable in 2012/13 exceeded £1,000.		✓

Tutorial note

The taxpayer must notify HMRC of any untaxed income received in 2013/14 by 5 October 2014.

The second statement is false because a taxpayer does not have to make payments on account if their tax payable is either:

- *no more than £1,000, or*
- *less than 20% of their income tax liability*

(c) The answer is C

Tutorial note

An AAT member has a professional duty to their client and to society as a whole.

(d) The answer is B

Tutorial note

An AAT member must not discuss his suspicions with the client as this is an offence called 'Tipping off'. He does not report his suspicions to HMRC or the AAT. He should report his suspicions to his MLRO.

TASK 8

HM Revenue & Customs

Employment

Tax year 6 April 2013 to 5 April 2014

Your name: TREVOR OLDHAM

Your Unique Taxpayer Reference (UTR):

Complete an *Employment* page for each employment or directorship

1 Pay from this employment – the total from your P45 or P60 – *before tax was taken off*

£ 25833.00

2 UK tax taken off pay in box 1

£ 3705.00

3 Tips and other payments not on your P60 – *read the Employment notes*

£ .00

4 PAYE tax reference of your employer (on your P45/P60)

/

5 Your employer's name

TARGET PLC

6 If you were a company director, put 'X' in the box

7 And, if the company was a close company, put 'X' in the box

8 If you are a part-time teacher in England or Wales and are on the Repayment of Teachers' Loans Scheme for this employment, put 'X' in the box

Benefits from your employment – use your form P11D (or equivalent information)

9 Company cars and vans – *the total 'cash equivalent' amount*

£ 4219.00

10 Fuel for company cars and vans – *the total 'cash equivalent' amount*

£ .00

11 Private medical and dental insurance – *the total 'cash equivalent' amount*

£ 300.00

12 Vouchers, credit cards and excess mileage allowance

£ .00

13 Goods and other assets provided by your employer – *the total value or amount*

£ .00

14 Accommodation provided by your employer – *the total value or amount*

£ .00

15 Other benefits (including interest-free and low interest loans) – *the total 'cash equivalent' amount*

£ .00

16 Expenses payments received and balancing charges

£ .00

Employment expenses

17 Business travel and subsistence expenses

£ .00

18 Fixed deductions for expenses

£ .00

19 Professional fees and subscriptions

£ 190.00

20 Other expenses and capital allowances

£ .00

Shares schemes, employment lump sums, compensation, deductions and Seafarers' Earnings Deduction are on the *Additional information* pages enclosed in the tax return pack.

SA102 2013 Page E 1 HMRC 12/12

Box 1 only 10 months salary plus commission

Box 9 only 10 months of car benefit

TASK 9

(a) The answer is C

	£
Proceeds	75,000
Less: Auction fees (£75,000 × 8%)	(6,000)
	69,000
Less: Cost £49,000 × (£75,000/(£75,000 + £125,000))	(18,375)
Chargeable gain	50,625

Tutorial note

If a taxpayer inherits an asset their cost for future capital gains disposals is the value at death; also referred to as the probate value.

Note that this rule is similar to receiving a gift where the cost is the market value at the date of receipt.

With a part disposal of the land, the cost must be apportioned using the A/A+B formula NOT on the proportion of acreage sold.

Note that A is the gross sale proceeds, before deducting the auction fees.

(b) The answer is D

	£
Proceeds	355,000
Less: Selling costs	(6,500)
	348,500
Less: Cost (£174,000 + £1,740)	(175,740)
Extension	(20,000)
Chargeable gain	152,760

Tutorial note

If a taxpayer sells an asset in an arm's length sale, as is the case with an auction, it does not matter that the market value may be different to the actual proceeds. The actual proceeds must be used in the computation.

Insurance premiums are not an allowable cost for capital gains purposes.

(c) This statement is false.

(d) Rose

(i)	Gain on racehorse	£Nil
(ii)	Allowable loss on antique table (W1)	£5,050
(iii)	Gain on holiday cottage (W2)	£52,000

Tutorial note

A racehorse is a wasting chattel and is exempt from capital gains tax.

Workings

(W1) **Antique table**

	£
Deemed proceeds	6,000
Less: Selling costs	(50)
	5,950
Less: Cost	(11,000)
Allowable loss	(5,050)

Tutorial note

An antique table is a non-wasting and as it cost > £6,000 and proceeds are < £6,000, special rules apply.

The gross proceeds are deemed to be £6,000 in the allowable loss calculation.

(W2) **Holiday cottage**

	£
Proceeds	110,000
Less: Cost	(50,000)
Extension	(8,000)
Chargeable gain	52,000

TASK 10

Chargeable gain calculation

	£
Proceeds (9,000 × £5)	45,000
Less: Cost (W)	(19,815)
Chargeable gain	25,185

***Working:* Share pool**

		Number	*Cost* £
Oct 2009	Purchase	1,000	1,250
Jan 2010	Purchase	3,000	6,300
		4,000	7,550
Dec 2011	Bonus issue (1 for 3)	1,333	Nil
Jan 2012	Purchase	5,000	15,200
		10,333	22,750
Oct 2013	Sale (£22,750 × 9,000/10,333)	(9,000)	(19,815)
Balance c/f		1,333	2,935

Tutorial note

The rights issue was not taken up by Paul and therefore should not be included in the share pool.

TASK 11

(a) The answer is A.

	£
Sale proceeds	336,000
Less: Cost	(101,000)
	235,000
Less: PPR relief (£235,000 × 230/254) (W)	(212,795)
Chargeable gain	22,205
Less: AE	(10,900)
Taxable gain	11,305

***Working:* PPR relief**

		Total months	*Exempt months*	*Chargeable months*
1.3.92 to 31.3.96	Owner occupied	49	49	
1.4.96 to 31.3.05	Working in Newcastle	108	84 (Note 1)	24
1.4.05 to 31.10.11	Owner occupied	79	79	
1.11.11 to 30.4.13	Empty	18	18 (Note 2)	
		254	230	24

Tutorial note

1 *Of the 108 months working in Newcastle, a maximum of 48 months are deemed occupation as "working elsewhere in the UK".*

A further 36 months are then allowed as deemed occupation for any reason – as this period is both preceded and followed by periods of actual occupation by Harold.

Total period of deemed occupation is therefore 84 months (48 + 36).

2 *The last 36 months of ownership is always allowed. Of the last 36 months, Harold actually occupied the property for 18 months; the remaining 18 months when the property is empty will also be exempt.*

(b) (i) **Taxable gain**

	£
Chargeable gains (£23,000 + £14,500)	37,500
Less: Current year allowable losses (Note)	(2,600)
	34,900
Less: Capital losses brought forward	(5,600)
Net chargeable gain	29,300
Less: Annual exempt amount	(10,900)
Taxable gain	18,400

(ii) **Capital loss left to carry forward**

Loss on disposal to brother (Note)	3,000

Tutorial note

The loss arising on the disposal to the brother is a connected person loss.

It cannot be set against other gains. It can only be carried forward and set against gains arising from disposals to the same brother in the future.

(c) (i) **Capital gains tax liability**

	£
Capital gains	26,000
Less: Annual exempt amount	(10,900)
Taxable gains	15,100

£		
2,010 (W)	× 18%	361.80
13,090	× 28%	3,665.20
15,100		4,027.00

Working

	£
Basic rate band	32,010
Less: Taxable income	(30,000)
Basic rate band unused	2,010

Tutorial note

Capital gains are taxed at 18% if they fall below the basic rate threshold and 28% if they fall above the threshold.

(ii) Due date of payment is 31 January 2015

Section 5

AQ2010: MOCK ASSESSMENT QUESTIONS

SECTION 1

TASK 1.1

Joachim asks whether the following statements are true or false.

Tick the correct box for each statement.

	True	False
An individual who does not receive a tax return must inform HMRC of any untaxed income received in 2013/14 by 31 December 2014.		
Payments on account are compulsory in 2013/14 for all taxpayers whose tax payable in 2012/13 exceeded £1,000.		

TASK 1.2

(a) Which ONE of the following statements is not correct?

A The AAT expects its members to maintain an objective outlook

B You must follow the rules of confidentiality even after a client relationship has ended

C An AAT member has a professional duty only to their client and not society as a whole

D An AAT member advising on tax issues has a duty to both their client and to HMRC

(b) If an AAT member suspects his client of money laundering which one of the following actions must he take?

A He should discuss his suspicions with the client

B He should report his suspicions to his employer's Money Laundering Reporting Officer

C He should report his suspicions to HMRC

D He should report his suspicions to the AAT

TASK 1.3

For each statement, tick either employment or self employment.

	Employment	Self employment
Being provided with paid holidays		
Having to correct poor work at your own expense		
Providing your own tools and equipment		

TASK 1.4

Joseph was born on 1 September 1961. In 2013/14 he received a salary of £51,000 until 31 December 2013 when he received a pay rise of 4%.

He received a bonus payment on 31 March 2013 of £8,000 relating to his employer's year ended 31 December 2012 and another payment on 31 March 2014 for £10,000 relating to his employer's year ended 31 December 2013.

There was no occupational pension scheme available with his employer so Joseph paid £720 into a private pension each month. He also contributed £100 a month to charity via the company's payroll giving scheme.

What is Joseph's taxable employment income for 2013/14?

A £49,510

B £60,310

C £51,670

C £58,310

TASK 1.5

Oliver Reeves was unemployed until 6 June 2013, when he started a new job as a salesman with an annual salary of £27,000.

As part of his remuneration package, he was provided with the following benefits:

- From 6 November 2013, a Ford Focus car. The list price of the car is £15,500 and Oliver paid his company £100 per month in respect of his private use of the car.
- The CO_2 emissions are 153 g/km and it has a diesel engine.
- The company pays for all the running costs of the car including the fuel. Oliver paid his company £30 per month towards the provision of diesel.
- From 6 December 2013, a second car for his wife. The list price of the car is £12,000; however the company bought it second hand for £9,000. The CO_2 emissions are 93 g/km.
- It has a petrol engine; but the company does not pay for any private fuel on this car.

(a)	What is the taxable benefit for the use of the Ford Focus?	£
(b)	What is the taxable benefit for the fuel provided by the company?	£
(c)	What is the scale charge percentage for Oliver's wife's car?	£
(d)	What price is used to calculate the car benefit on Oliver's wife's car?	£

TASK 1.6

What is the taxable benefit for each of the employment benefits received by the employees listed below?

(a)	Tracey drove 8,000 business miles and 2,000 personal miles in 2013/14, she uses her own car. Her employer pays her 49p per business mile.	£
(b)	Carol, a basic rate taxpayer, receives £55 per week in childcare vouchers from her employer. The vouchers are for a registered child care provider.	£
(c)	Bill received £1,800 as a loan from his employer in 2013/14. He pays interest on the loan at the rate of 2%.	£
(d)	Les borrowed a digital camera from his employer on 6 June 2013 until 5 April 2014 to use on his holidays and for family occasions. The market value of the camera on 6 June 2013 was £1,200.	£
(e)	From 6 January 2014, Sarah was provided with a company loan of £20,000 on which she pays interest at 2.5% per annum.	£

TASK 1.7

Rose has asked you to advise her which of the following benefits, provided to employees earning over £12,000 per year, are exempt.

	Exempt	Not exempt
Use of a company car with CO_2 emissions of 72 g/km		
A place in the company's workplace based nursery for two children		
One mobile telephone for each employee and each spouse		
Provision of bicycle helmets for staff earning below £20,000 p.a.		
Staff Christmas party costing £75 per employee		
Relocation expenses of £7,500		

TASK 1.8

Read the following statements about expense payments and tick the relevant box to mark each one as true or false.

	True	False
In order for employment expenses to be deductible from employment income, they just need to be incurred wholly and exclusively in the performance of the employment duties.		
Martin is employed as an information technology consultant. He pays £1,020 per annum in subscriptions of which £580 is paid to the Chartered Institute of Information Technology and £440 to his local golf club where he often meets clients for lunch and a round of golf. Both subscriptions can be deducted from Martin's employment income for tax purposes.		

Sam has to travel 10 miles per day to get to and from his place of employment. Twice a week he has to go to a client for the day and he usually does not go into his normal office on those days. He cannot claim the cost of travel to and from his normal place of work but he can claim as a deduction from his employment income the cost of travel to the client, provided he deducts his normal commuting mileage from his claim.		
Krista makes a donation to charity under the Gift aid scheme. The donation needs to be grossed up at 100/80 and then deducted in her employment income computation.		

TASK 1.9

(a) Place the following types of investment income in the correct column in the table below.

- Premium Bond prize
- Interest from 3½% War loan (a government stock)
- Bank interest received
- Interest from NS&I income bonds
- Interest from an ISA
- Interest from an NS&I bank account

Received net	**Received gross**	**Exempt**

(b) During 2013/14, Lexie received interest of £240 from her building society account and £370 from her NS&I Direct Saver account

The tax deducted from this interest totals:

A £48.00

B £60.00

C £122.00

D £152.50

TASK 1.10

In 2013/14, Joe received £13,500 dividends from his investments in UK companies and £2,700 from investments in his stocks and shares ISA.

He has other taxable income of £142,000.

What is the tax liability arising on his dividend income?

TASK 1.11

Jason received NS&I interest of £150 and won £20,000 on a National Lottery scratch card in 2013/14.

How much of this income should he enter into his income tax computation?

A £150 for NS&I and £20,000 for the winnings

B £187 for NS&I and £Nil for the winnings

C £150 for NS&I and £Nil for the winnings

D £187 for NS&I and £20,000 for the winnings

TASK 1.12

Rita, aged 36, is employed as a receptionist with a gross annual salary of £51,000. On 21 April 2013 she received a bonus of £4,220 which related to her performance during the year ended 31 March 2013.

She was provided with accommodation by her employer. The house has an annual value £4,200 and the employer pays a rent of £250 per month. Her employer also paid a utility bill for the house of £180 during 2013/14. She moved out when she left her employment on 5 December 2013.

She has not found another job.

Rita received building society interest of £1,800 and ISA interest of £105.

Use the table below to calculate Rita's income tax liability for 2013/14.

TASK 1.13

Katie has written to you with the following query:

> 'Please can you explain to me how my tax payments are calculated as I do not understand what needs paying and when?
>
> My income tax liability was £8,900 for 2012/13. According to your latest calculation my income tax liability will be £10,200 for 2013/14. In addition I have to pay capital gains tax of £3,350 in respect of capital disposals made in 2013/14.
>
> Could you please let me know what I should pay and the due dates for payment?
>
> Many thanks
>
> Katie

You need to respond appropriately to her query.

TASK 1.14

Complete the tax return below as far as the following information permits.

Trevor Oldham was employed from 1 June 2013 as a salesman by Target plc. His gross annual salary was £28,000 and he received commission of £2,500 in 2013/14. PAYE of £3,705 was deducted from his salary.

He was provided with a company car from 1 July 2013 with an annual benefit value of £5,625.

He was also provided with private medical insurance which cost his employer £300 in 2013/14. Trevor paid a £190 subscription to his trade association.

Employment

Tax year 6 April 2013 to 5 April 2014

Your name

Your Unique Taxpayer Reference (UTR)

Complete an *Employment* page for each employment or directorship

1 Pay from this employment - the total from your P45 or P60 - *before tax was taken off*

£ .00

2 UK tax taken off pay in box 1

£ .00

3 Tips and other payments not on your P60 - *read the Employment notes*

£ .00

4 PAYE tax reference of your employer (on your P45/P60)

/

5 Your employer's name

6 If you were a company director, put 'X' in the box

7 And, if the company was a close company, put 'X' in the box

8 If you are a part-time teacher in England or Wales and are on the Repayment of Teachers' Loans Scheme for this employment, put 'X' in the box

Benefits from your employment - use your form P11D (or equivalent information)

9 Company cars and vans - *the total 'cash equivalent' amount*

£ .00

10 Fuel for company cars and vans - *the total 'cash equivalent' amount*

£ .00

11 Private medical and dental insurance - *the total 'cash equivalent' amount*

£ .00

12 Vouchers, credit cards and excess mileage allowance

£ .00

13 Goods and other assets provided by your employer - *the total value or amount*

£ .00

14 Accommodation provided by your employer - *the total value or amount*

£ .00

15 Other benefits (including interest-free and low interest loans) - *the total 'cash equivalent' amount*

£ .00

16 Expenses payments received and balancing charges

£ .00

Employment expenses

17 Business travel and subsistence expenses

£ .00

18 Fixed deductions for expenses

£ .00

19 Professional fees and subscriptions

£ .00

20 Other expenses and capital allowances

£ .00

Shares schemes, employment lump sums, compensation, deductions and Seafarers' Earnings Deduction are on the *Additional information* pages enclosed in the tax return pack.

SA102 2013 Page E 1 HMRC 12/12

SECTION 2

TASK 2.1

Is the following statement true or is it false?

Wear and tear allowance is calculated as:

10% (Rents received – Water rates and council tax paid by the landlord)

TASK 2.2

Steven Mason has three properties, details of which are as follows:

Four bedroom house:

1 This furnished house is rented out for £780 per month. The property was occupied throughout 2013/14. Steven paid council tax of £800 and water rates of £300 for 2013/14.

2 The only other expense paid by Steven in respect of the house was 7% commission to the agent on the rent received.

One bedroom flat:

3 This unfurnished flat is rented out for £415 per month. The property was occupied until 5 November 2013 when the tenants moved out without paying the last month's rent. It is highly unlikely that Steven will be able to recover this debt. New tenants moved in on 6 January 2014 when the rent had increased to £435 per month.

4 Steven paid a cleaner £60 per month to clean this property throughout 2013/14.

Two bedroom house:

5 This house was rented out from 6 July 2013 for £610 per month. Steven purchased furniture for £5,000 to go in the house.

6 Steven paid council tax of £700 and £225 water rates in respect of the house for 2013/14. He also paid interest of £280.

Calculate the profit or loss made on each property using the following table.

	Four bedroom house £	*One bedroom flat* £	*Two bedroom house* £
Income:			
Expenses:			

TASK 2.3

Which of the following statements are true or false?

Tick the correct box for each statement.

	True	False
The amount of rent you can receive which is tax free under the rent-a-room scheme is £4,500.		
The rent-a-room limit is compared to the gross rents before deduction of expenses.		
A husband and wife jointly owning a property cannot have a rent-a-room limit each to match against a lodger's rental income. However, if two friends purchase a house together and rent to a lodger, they can have a rent-a-room limit each.		

TASK 2.4

For each statement, tick the appropriate box.

	Actual proceeds used	Market value used	No gain / no loss basis
(a) Neena sells an asset to her aunt for a price fixed by Neena's accountant			
(b) Jacob gives an asset to his friend Agnes			
(c) Christina sells an asset to her ex husband Owen.			

TASK 2.5

(a) Paul inherited seven acres of land in August 2010 from his grandfather.

The land had cost his grandfather £15,000 but was worth £49,000 (the probate value) when Paul received it.

Paul sold three acres in November 2013 for £75,000 when the remaining four acres were worth £125,000. He paid auctioneer's commission of 8% when he sold the asset.

What is the gain on this asset?

A £51,572

B £48,000

C £50,625

D £63,375

(b) Artem bought a holiday home in March 2009 for £174,000 plus stamp duty of £1,740.

She spent £20,000 on extending the property in April 2011. She has paid insurance premiums totalling £3,750 during the time she has owned the asset.

She sold the property at auction for £355,000 in March 2014 incurring selling costs of £6,500. Artem was disappointed with this price as the property had been valued at £400,000 before the auction.

What is the gain on this asset?

A £149,010

B £197,760

C £154,500

D £152,760

(c) True or false:

Accountancy fees for calculating capital gains tax are an allowable selling expense when disposing of an asset.

TASK 2.6

Paul disposed of 9,000 shares in Sun Ltd for £5 per share in October 2013.

He acquired the shares as follows:

		Number of shares	*Cost*
October 2009	Purchase	1,000	£1,250
January 2010	Purchase	3,000	£6,300
December 2011	Bonus issue	1 for 3	
January 2012	Purchase	5,000	£15,200

In June 2011, Sun Ltd had a rights issue of 1 for 5 shares for £2.25 per share. Paul did not take up the rights shares.

Clearly showing the balance of shares, and their value, to carry forward calculate the gain or loss made on these shares.

All workings must be shown in your calculations.

TASK 2.7

Rose disposed of the following assets in 2013/14.

For each asset, calculate the gain before annual exempt amount or the allowable loss:

(a)	Sold a racehorse for £25,000. She had originally purchased the racehorse for £8,900.	£
(b)	Sold an antique table to her neighbour for £5,000. She paid £50 commission on the sale. She originally purchased the table for £11,000. The table got scratched while she owned it (hence the low proceeds).	£
(c)	Sold a holiday cottage in Devon for £110,000. She originally purchased the cottage for £50,000 and extended it two years later which cost £8,000.	£
(d)	Sold a third interest in a painting for £12,320. She originally purchased the painting for £14,118. The value of the other two thirds interest in at the date of sale was £22,150.	£

TASK 2.8

Harold bought a house for £101,000 on 1 March 1992.

He lived in the house with his wife until 31 March 1996 when they went to work in Newcastle.

He returned to the house on 1 April 2005 and lived in it until 31 October 2011 when he moved in with his elderly parents.

The house was sold for £336,000 on 1 May 2013.

What is the taxable gain assuming Harold has no other disposals in 2013/14?

A £11,305

B £235,000

C £44,612

D £22,205

E £212,795

TASK 2.9

Margaret has disposed of several capital assets in 2013/14 and realised the following gains and losses:

	Disposal to:	£
Chargeable gain	Aunt	23,000
Chargeable gain	Unconnected person	14,500
Allowable loss	Brother	(3,000)
Allowable loss	Friend	(2,600)

Margaret has unutilised capital losses relating to 2012/13 of £5,600.

(a)	What are Margaret's taxable gains for 2013/14?	£
(b)	What is the capital loss remaining to carry forward to 2014/15?	£

Section 6

AQ2010: MOCK ASSESSMENT ANSWERS

SECTION 1

TASK 1.1

	True	False
An individual who does not receive a tax return must inform HMRC of any untaxed income received in 2012/13 by 31 December 2014.		✓
Payments on account are compulsory in 2013/14 for all taxpayers whose tax payable in 2012/13 exceeded £1,000.		✓

Tutorial note

The taxpayer must notify HMRC of any untaxed income received in 2013/14 by 5 October 2014.

The second statement is false because a taxpayer does not have to make payments on account if their tax payable is either:

- *no more than £1,000, or*
- *less than 20% of their income tax liability*
  (or, to put it another way, 80% of their tax liability is covered by deduction of tax at source).

TASK 1.2

(a) The answer is C

Tutorial note

An AAT member has a professional duty to their client and to society as a whole.

(b) The answer is B

Tutorial note

An AAT member must not discuss his suspicions with the client as this is an offence called 'Tipping off'. He does not report his suspicions to HMRC or the AAT. He should report his suspicions to his MLRO.

TASK 1.3

	Employment	**Self employment**
Being provided with paid holidays	✓	
Having to correct poor work at your own expense		✓
Providing your own tools and equipment		✓

Key answer tips

You need to make sure that you know the factors that HMRC will consider to decide the status of an individual with regard to employment or self employment.

TASK 1.4

The answer is B

	£
Salary (£51,000 × 9/12) + (£51,000 × 1.04% × 3/12)	51,510
Bonus received in 2013/14	10,000
Less: Payroll giving contribution	(1,200)
Taxable employment income	60,310

Tutorial note

The tax year runs from 6 April 2013 to 5 April 2014 and Joseph's salary changes after nine months of this period. The salary must therefore be time apportioned.

The bonus is assessed in the tax year of receipt.

Unlike contributions into an occupational pension scheme, contributions into a personal pension scheme are not an allowable deduction from employment income.

Instead, relief for basic rate tax is given at source and higher rate (and additional rate relief, if applicable) is given by extending the basic rate and higher rate band thresholds by the gross personal pension contribution.

The contribution to charity under the payroll giving scheme is an allowable deduction from employment income.

TASK 1.5

(a) **Ford Focus**

CO_2 emissions are rounded down to 150 g/km.

Appropriate percentage = (14% diesel + (150 – 95) × 1/5) = 25%

Car has been available for 5 months of the tax year.

	£
£15,500 × 25% × 5/12	1,615
Less: Contribution in respect of private use (£100 × 5 months)	(500)
Car benefit	1,115

Tutorial note

The car has CO_2 emissions in excess of 94 g/km.

The appropriate percentage is therefore calculated in the normal way (i.e. a scale percentage of 11% for petrol cars and 14% for diesel cars, plus 1% for each complete 5 g/km above 95 g/km up to a maximum percentage of 35%).

As the car has not been available all year, the benefit must be time apportioned.

Contributions in respect of the private use of the car are an allowable deduction from the benefit.

(b) **Ford Focus**

Fuel benefit = (£21,100 × 25% × 5/12) = £2,198

Tutorial note

The appropriate percentage for the fuel benefit is the same as that calculated for the car benefit. This is applied to a fixed scale figure of £21,100.

As the car has not been available all year, the benefit must be time apportioned.

A contribution towards the provision of private petrol is not an allowable deduction from the benefit.

(c) **Oliver's wife's car**

Appropriate percentage = 10%.

Tutorial note

The car has CO_2 emissions of between 76 and 94 g/km and is therefore a low emission car.

The appropriate percentage for a petrol car is 10%, and 13% for a diesel car.

(d) **Oliver's wife's car**

Price used to calculate the car benefit = £12,000.

Tutorial note

The second hand price actually paid by the company is not relevant. The car benefit is based on the original manufacturer's list price.

TASK 1.6

(a)	Tracey drove 8,000 business miles and 2,000 personal miles in 2013/14, she uses her own car. Her employer pays her 36p per business mile.	£320
(b)	Carol, a basic rate taxpayer, receives £55 per week in childcare vouchers from her employer. The vouchers are for a registered child care provider.	£Nil
(c)	Bill received £1,800 as a loan from his employer in 2013/14. He pays interest on the loan at the rate of 2%.	£Nil
(d)	Les borrowed a digital camera from his employer on 6 June 2013 until 5 April 2014 to use on his holidays and for family occasions. The market value of the camera on 6 June 2013 was £1,200.	£200
(e)	From 6 January 2014, Sarah received a company loan of £20,000 on which she pays interest at 2.5% per annum.	£75

Workings

(a) **Use of own car**

	£
Amount received from company (8,000 × 49p)	3,920
Allowable under HMRC rules:	
8,000 × 45p	(3,600)
Taxable benefit	320

(b) **Childcare vouchers**

Taxable benefit = £Nil

Tutorial note

Childcare vouchers up to £55 per week spent with an approved child minder are an exempt benefit for a basic rate taxpayer.

(c) **Company loan**

Taxable benefit = £Nil

Tutorial note

Loans which do not exceed £5,000 at any time in the tax year are an exempt benefit.

(d) **Use of camera**

Taxable benefit = (£1,200 × 20% × 10/12) = £200

Tutorial note

The benefit for the use of a company asset such as a camera is 20% of the market value of the asset when first made available to the employee.

As the camera was only made available to Les from 6 June 2013, the benefit is time apportioned.

(e) **Company loan**

Taxable benefit = (£20,000 × (4% – 2.5%) × 3/12) = £75

Tutorial note

Beneficial loan interest benefit is calculated as follows:

= Outstanding loan × the difference between the official rate of interest (4% in 2013/14) and the actual interest rate paid by the employee.

However, as the loan was provided nine months into the tax year 2013/14, the benefit must be time apportioned as the rates of interest quoted are annual rates of interest.

TASK 1.7

	Exempt	Not exempt
Use of a company car with CO_2 emissions of 72 g/km		✓
A place in the company's workplace based nursery for two children	✓	
One mobile telephone for each employee and each spouse		✓
Provision of bicycle helmets for staff earning below £20,000 p.a.		✓
Staff Christmas party costing £75 per employee	✓	
Relocation expenses of £7,500	✓	

Tutorial note

A car with CO_2 emissions of less than 75 g/km is a "very low emission car". The provision of such a car is not however an exempt benefit. The appropriate % will be 5% for a petrol car and 8% for a diesel car.

A place in the workplace nursery is an exempt benefit, regardless of the number of children or cost of provision. The limits that apply depending on the rate at which the employee pays tax relate to childcare vouchers and childcare with approved carers other than in the workplace nursery.

Only one mobile phone per employee is treated as an exempt benefit.

The provision of cycle helmets is an exempt benefit provided they are available to all staff generally. It will not be exempt if it is conditional on the amount earned.

Staff entertaining of up to £150 per head per tax year is an exempt benefit.

Relocation expenses of up to £8,000 are an exempt benefit.

TASK 1.8

	True	False
In order for employment expenses to be deductible from employment income, they just need to be incurred wholly and exclusively in the performance of the employment duties.		✓
Martin is employed as an information technology consultant. He pays £1,020 per annum in subscriptions of which £580 is paid to the Chartered Institute of Information Technology and £440 to his local golf club where he often meets clients for lunch and a round of golf. Both subscriptions can be deducted from Martin's employment income for tax purposes.		✓
Sam has to travel 10 miles per day to get to and from his place of employment. Twice a week he has to go to a client for the day and he usually does not go into his normal office on those days. He cannot claim the cost of travel to and from his normal place of work but he can claim as a deduction from his employment income the cost of travel to the client, provided he deducts his normal commuting mileage from his claim.		✓
Krista makes a donation to charity under the Gift Aid scheme. The donation needs to be grossed up at 100/80 and then deducted in her employment income computation.		✓

Tutorial note

To be allowable for employment income purposes, expenses have to be incurred wholly, exclusively ***and necessarily*** *in the performance of employment duties.*

The donation to the Chartered Institute of Information Technology will be an allowable deduction for employment income purposes. However, the golf membership will not be allowable for tax, despite there being a work related purpose for visiting the golf club.

Mileage to a temporary place of work is allowable in full. There is no need to deduct the mileage of ordinary commuting from the expense claim.

A donation to charity via a company's authorised payroll giving scheme is an allowable deduction from employment income.

However, donations under the Gift Aid scheme are not relieved against employment income. Instead, basic rate relief is given at source. Higher rate relief (and if applicable, additional rate relief) is given by extending the basic rate and higher rate band thresholds by the gross Gift Aid payment.

TASK 1.9

(a) **Sources of income**

Received net	Received gross	Exempt
Bank interest received	Interest from 3½% war loan Interest from NS&I income bonds Interest from an NS&I bank account	Premium Bond prize Interest from an ISA

(b) The answer is B

Tutorial note

NS&I interest is received gross.

The building society interest is received net of 20% tax.

Hence the tax deducted = (£240 × 20/80) = £60.00

TASK 1.10

Income tax on dividend income

	£
Other taxable income	142,000
Dividend income:	
From UK companies (£13,500 × 100/90)	15,000
From stocks and shares ISA – exempt income	Nil
Total income = Net income = Adjusted net income	157,000
Less: Personal allowance (Note)	(Nil)
Taxable income	157,000

Income tax on dividend income only: (Note)	
(£150,000 – £142,000) = £8,000 × 32.5%	2,600.00
(£157,000 – £150,000) = £7,000 × 37.5%	2,625.00
Income tax liability on dividend income	5,225.00

Tutorial note

As Joe's adjusted net income exceeds £118,880, he will not be entitled to any personal allowance. Furthermore, as his taxable income exceeds £150,000, Joe is an additional rate taxpayer.

Dividends that fall into the higher rate band will be taxed at 32.5%. Dividends that fall above £150,000 will be taxed at 37.5%.

TASK 1.11

The answer is C.

Tutorial note

NS&I interest is received gross and scratch card winnings are exempt from income tax.

TASK 1.12

Rita – Income tax computation – 2013/14

	Total	*Other*	*Savings*
	£	£	£
Salary (£51,000 × 8/12)	34,000		
Bonus (received 21 April 2013)	4,220		
Accommodation benefit (W)	2,980		
	———		
Employment income	41,200	41,200	
BSI (£1,800 × 100/80)	2,250		2,250
ISA interest – exempt	Nil		
	———	———	———
Net income	43,450	41,200	2,250
Less: PA	(9,440)	(9,440)	
	———	———	———
Taxable income	34,010	31,760	2,250
	———	———	———

Income tax:		
Other income	31,760 at 20%	6,352.00
Savings	250 at 20%	50.00
	———	
	32,010	
Savings	2,000 at 40%	800.00
	———	
	34,010	
	———	———
Income tax liability		7,202.00
		———

Working **– Accommodation benefit:**

	£
Higher of:	
(i) Annual value = £4,200	
(ii) Rent paid by employer = (£250 × 12) = £3,000	
Only available for 8 months of the year:	
Basic charge benefit = (£4,200 × 8/12)	2,800
Utility bill paid for by employer – benefit = cost to employer	180
	———
Total accommodation benefit	2,980
	———

Key answer tips

It is important when using this type of layout to analyse the taxable income into "other income", "savings" and "dividends" as different rates of tax apply to the different sources of income.

Note that:

- the above layout should be possible as the CBT should give five columns to complete the calculation
- the total lines do not have to be inserted in the real CBT
- you may find it useful to do the computation on paper first before inputting on screen
- it is acceptable to have the total column at the end rather than the beginning if you prefer. However, we recommend that the analysis columns are in the fixed order: "other income", "savings" and then "dividends", as this is the order in which they must be taxed through the bands.

TASK 1.13

Dear Katie,

Payments on account of the tax liability for any year are paid by 31 January in that tax year, and by 31 July following the tax year. This is based on an estimate, using the preceding tax years' payable.

Therefore, when you made your tax payments on 31 January 2013 and 31 July 2013 for 2012/13, this was based on your liability for 2011/12.

When the final figures are sent to HMRC, if these two instalments are not enough to cover the full liability, a balancing payment is due on 31 January following the tax year.

For 2013/14 your payments due will therefore be:

31 January 2014	(£8,900 × 1/2)	£4,450
31 July 2014	(£8,900 × 1/2)	£4,450
31 January 2015	(£10,200 – £8,900)	£1,300

In addition, on 31 January 2015, all of the capital gains tax liability of £3,350 is due for payment as capital gains tax is never paid in instalments.

Finally on 31 January 2015 you will have to make the first payment on account of your 2014/15 liability. This will be £5,100 as it is based on half of your 2013/14 liability of £10,200.

The total amount due on 31 January 2015 will be £9,750 (£1,300 + £3,350 + £5,100).

I hope this makes things clearer. If you have any queries please do not hesitate to contact me.

Best regards

AAT Student

TASK 1.14

HM Revenue & Customs

Employment

Tax year 6 April 2013 to 5 April 2014

Your name: TREVOR OLDHAM

Your Unique Taxpayer Reference (UTR):

Complete an *Employment* page for each employment or directorship

1 Pay from this employment – the total from your P45 or P60 – *before tax was taken off*

£ 25833.00

2 UK tax taken off pay in box 1

£ 3705.00

3 Tips and other payments not on your P60 – *read the Employment notes*

£ .00

4 PAYE tax reference of your employer (on your P45/P60)

/

5 Your employer's name

TARGET PLC

6 If you were a company director, put 'X' in the box

7 And, if the company was a close company, put 'X' in the box

8 If you are a part-time teacher in England or Wales and are on the Repayment of Teachers' Loans Scheme for this employment, put 'X' in the box

Benefits from your employment – use your form P11D (or equivalent information)

9 Company cars and vans – *the total 'cash equivalent' amount*

£ 4219.00

10 Fuel for company cars and vans – *the total 'cash equivalent' amount*

£ .00

11 Private medical and dental insurance – *the total 'cash equivalent' amount*

£ 300.00

12 Vouchers, credit cards and excess mileage allowance

£ .00

13 Goods and other assets provided by your employer – *the total value or amount*

£ .00

14 Accommodation provided by your employer – *the total value or amount*

£ .00

15 Other benefits (including interest-free and low interest loans) – *the total 'cash equivalent' amount*

£ .00

16 Expenses payments received and balancing charges

£ .00

Employment expenses

17 Business travel and subsistence expenses

£ .00

18 Fixed deductions for expenses

£ .00

19 Professional fees and subscriptions

£ 190.00

20 Other expenses and capital allowances

£ .00

Shares schemes, employment lump sums, compensation, deductions and Seafarers' Earnings Deduction are on the *Additional information* pages enclosed in the tax return pack.

SA102 2013 Page E 1 HMRC 12/12

Box 1 only 10 months salary plus commission

Box 9 only 10 months of car benefit

SECTION 2

TASK 2.1

The statement is true.

TASK 2.2

	Four bedroom house	*One bedroom flat*	*Two bedroom house*
	£	£	£
Income:			
(£780 × 12 months)	9,360		
(£415 × 7 months)		2,905	
(£435 × 3 months)		1,305	
Less: Bad debt (Note)		(415)	
		3,795	
(£610 × 9 months)			5,490
Expenses:			
Council tax	(800)		(700)
Water rates	(300)		(225)
Agents commission (7% × £9,360)	(655)		
Cleaning		(720)	
Interest			(280)
Wear and tear allowance			
(£9,360 – £800 – £300) × 10%	(826)		
(£5,490 – £700 – £225) × 10%			(457)
Rental profit	6,779	3,075	3,828

Tutorial note

Rental income is assessed on an accruals basis; therefore all of the rent accrued should be brought into the computation.

However, there is relief for the rent which is irrecoverable. It can be deducted as a bad debt.

Note that if in the CBT there is a proforma already set up with narrative, and there is no bad debt line, it is acceptable to just include in the rental income section the net rents actually received rather than two entries of rents accrued and the bad debt deduction.

A wear and tear allowance is given for furnished properties.

The allowance available is:

10% × (Rent received – Water rates and council tax paid by the landlord)

TASK 2.3

	True	False
The amount of rent you can receive which is tax free under the rent-a-room scheme is £4,500.		✓
The rent-a-room limit is compared to the gross rents before deduction of expenses.	✓	
A husband and wife jointly owning a property cannot have a rent-a-room limit each to match against a lodger's rental income. However, if two friends purchase a house together and rent to a lodger, they can have a rent-a-room limit each.		✓

Tutorial note

The tax free limit for rent-a-room relief is £4,250 for 2013/14, not £4,500.

Only one rent-a-room relief limit is available per residential property lived in as a home.

It is not therefore possible to have two rent-a-room limits for a house, regardless of whether or not the owners of the property are married.

TASK 2.4

	Actual proceeds used	Market value used	No gain / no loss basis
(a) Neena sells an asset to her aunt for a price fixed by Neena's accountant	✓		
(b) Jacob gives an asset to his friend Agnes		✓	
(c) Christina sells an asset to her ex husband Owen.	✓		

Tutorial note

An aunt and an ex husband are not connected persons.

Gifts are always treated as disposals at market value.

TASK 2.5

(a) The answer is C

	£
Proceeds	75,000
Less: Auction fees (£75,000 × 8%)	(6,000)
	69,000
Less: Cost £49,000 × (£75,000/(£75,000 + £125,000))	(18,375)
Chargeable gain	50,625

Tutorial note

If a taxpayer inherits an asset their cost for future capital gains disposals is the value at death; also referred to as the probate value.

Note that this rule is similar to receiving a gift where the cost is the market value at the date of receipt.

With a part disposal of the land, the cost must be apportioned using the A/A+B formula NOT on the proportion of acreage sold.

Note that A is the gross sale proceeds, before deducting the auction fees.

(b) The answer is D

	£
Proceeds	355,000
Less: Selling costs	(6,500)
	348,500
Less: Cost (£174,000 + £1,740)	(175,740)
Extension	(20,000)
Chargeable gain	152,760

Tutorial note

If a taxpayer sells an asset in an arm's length sale, as is the case with an auction, it does not matter that the market value may be different to the actual proceeds. The actual proceeds must be used in the computation.

Insurance premiums are not an allowable cost for capital gains purposes.

(c) This statement is false.

TASK 2.6

Chargeable gain calculation

	£
Proceeds (9,000 × £5)	45,000
Less: Cost (W)	(19,815)
Chargeable gain	25,185

***Working:* Share pool**

		Number	*Cost* £
Oct 2009	Purchase	1,000	1,250
Jan 2010	Purchase	3,000	6,300
		4,000	7,550
Dec 2011	Bonus issue (1 for 3)	1,333	Nil
Jan 2012	Purchase	5,000	15,200
		10,333	22,750
Oct 2013	Sale (£22,750 × 9,000/10,333)	(9,000)	(19,815)
Balance c/f		1,333	2,935

Tutorial note

The rights issue was not taken up by Paul and therefore should not be included in the share pool.

TASK 2.7

(a)	Gain on racehorse	£Nil
(b)	Allowable loss on antique table (W1)	£5,050
(c)	Gain on holiday cottage (W2)	£52,000
(d)	Gain on painting (W3)	£7,274

Tutorial note

A racehorse is a wasting chattel and is exempt from capital gains tax.

Workings

(W1) **Antique table**

	£
Deemed proceeds	6,000
Less: Selling costs	(50)
	5,950
Less: Cost	(11,000)
Allowable loss	(5,050)

Tutorial note

An antique table is a non-wasting and as it cost > £6,000 and proceeds are < £6,000, special rules apply.

The gross proceeds are deemed to be £6,000 in the allowable loss calculation.

(W2) **Holiday cottage**

	£
Proceeds	110,000
Less: Cost	(50,000)
Extension	(8,000)
Chargeable gain	52,000

(W3) **Interest in a painting**

	£
Proceeds	12,320
Less: Cost £14,118 × (£12,320 / £12,320 + £22,150)	(5,046)
Chargeable gain	7,274

Tutorial note

The disposal of an interest in a painting is a part disposal and the normal A / (A + B) rules apply.

The special marginal relief rules do not apply as both the cost and the combined value of the painting (A + B), exceed £6,000.

TASK 2.8

The answer is A.

	£
Sale proceeds	336,000
Less: Cost	(101,000)
	235,000
Less: PPR relief (£235,000 × 230/254) (W)	(212,795)
Chargeable gain	22,205
Less: AE	(10,900)
Taxable gain	11,305

***Working:* PPR relief**

		Total months	*Exempt months*	*Chargeable months*
1.3.92 to 31.3.96	Owner occupied	49	49	
1.4.96 to 31.3.05	Working in Newcastle	108	84 (Note 1)	24
1.4.05 to 31.10.11	Owner occupied	79	79	
1.11.11 to 30.4.13	Empty	18	18 (Note 2)	
		254	230	24

Tutorial note

1 *Of the 108 months working in Newcastle, a maximum of 48 months are deemed occupation as "working elsewhere in the UK".*

A further 36 months are then allowed as deemed occupation for any reason – as this period is both preceded and followed by periods of actual occupation by Harold.

Total period of deemed occupation is therefore 84 months (48 + 36).

2 *The last 36 months of ownership is always allowed. Of the last 36 months, Harold actually occupied the property for 18 months; the remaining 18 months when the property is empty will also be exempt.*

TASK 2.9

(a) **Taxable gain**

	£
Chargeable gains (£23,000 + £14,500)	37,500
Less: Current year allowable losses (Note)	(2,600)
	34,900
Less: Capital losses brought forward	(5,600)
Net chargeable gain	29,300
Less: Annual exempt amount	(10,900)
Taxable gain	18,400

(b) **Capital loss left to carry forward**

Loss on disposal to brother (Note)	3,000

Tutorial note

The loss arising on the disposal to the brother is a connected person loss.

It cannot be set against other gains. It can only be carried forward and set against gains arising from disposals to the same brother in the future.